UNDERSTAND THE TIMES

A Simplified Biblical Perspective

T. A. McMAHON
ROGER OAKLAND

T.W.F.T. Publishers
Costa Mesa, California 92628

UNDERSTAND THE TIMES--A Simplified Biblical Perspective

Copyright © 1990 T.A. McMahon and Roger Oakland and published by T.W.F.T. Publishers, P.O. Box 8000, Costa Mesa, California 92628.

McMahon, T.A.
    Understand The Times, A Simplified Biblical Perspective

        1. Prophecy--Bible.   2. Bible--Study.

I. Oakland, Roger.   II. Title.

ISBN 0-936728-38-8

Printed in the United States of America.

Contents

UNDERSTAND THE TIMES

By: T.A. McMahon & Roger Oakland

Preface

This book is not intended to be a lengthy analysis of every detail of the "end times." It is not a heavily documented manuscript uncovering hidden teachings secretly written down by people no one ever heard of for their own inner group of disciples. Nor is it a collection of bizarre events from society's fringe elements normally assigned to the *National Enquirer*.

What we have in mind here is more like two men standing on the side of a busy highway, jumping up and down while pointing to the surrounding billboards which blatantly proclaim: the bridge is out down the road.

Actually, one of the men is jumping up and down, the other is handing out detour maps (Bibles).

We are concerned that many today are missing the larger than life signs which, according to the Bible, indicate that mankind is heading down a path of ultimate destruction. Equally troubling is the prevailing attitude of many travelers along this road who have glanced up at the billboards, yet continue on in the presumption the bridge will be fixed by the time they get there. There are, as well, those racing by, hanging out their car windows shouting "Not to worry, the potential is within us all to walk on water!" This highway is jammed with non-Christians and Christians alike.

Our objective is to evaluate many of the seductive anti-Biblical activities taking place today in the hope of helping our readers comprehend the practical consequences on their lives now and in the days ahead.

We want them to be informed of the Biblical perspective regarding the present and the future. The Biblical mandate is very clear: it is possible to understand such things; God wants us to know such things; He wants us to do certain things. God loves us and desires His best for us.

In all that is going on today we see an alarming trend among Biblical Christians toward drawing away from what ought to be their greatest longing: the joyous expectancy of the Groom, Jesus Christ, coming for His Bride, the Church. We hope that what is presented in the following pages will help to reverse such a trend.

Our prayer regarding this book is that it will encourage its readers to look to Christ and His Word as their life's chief resource, and to look for, as their heart's greatest desire, His soon return.

The Authors

1 ——————————————————

The Great Hope In Human Potential

There is a hope today that is capturing the hearts and minds of tens of millions of people the world over. The hope is that mankind will band together and begin to solve the world's problems that threaten not only the quality of life, but the very existence of life.

The problems, to one degree or another, have plagued the world throughout history. Yet it seems that unless this generation makes a concerted effort to solve them now, they will increase beyond the capacity of any future generation to deal with them effectively. Consider the following:

Wars have always been a part of history. A war today, however, has the potential for destroying all life on earth. Even minor wars can be the catalyst for drawing other countries into a world conflict of total annihilation.

Polluting the environment is not new for man, but there are now over 5 billion of us around (as opposed to about a billion and a half prior to the turn of the century) to contribute to the problem. Pollution's very visible impact has now reached critical levels, poisoning life the world over.

Nearly 13 million people died from starvation between 1960 and 1983. Yet for those who manage to survive a famine, the long-term effect is also devastating. Malnutrition resulting from food shortages in highly populated countries is creating generations of millions of physically and mentally weakened offspring.

Deadly diseases, once thought to have been all but vanquished by twentieth century science, have made an astonishing comeback. New drug-resistant strains along with new diseases such as AIDS are creating global epidemics.

Newspapers and magazines abound with headlines of concern regarding: the world's shrinking forests, the energy crisis, problems of nuclear power, toxic waste disposal, ozone depletion, the greenhouse effect, the third world debt crisis, and so on.

Given these rather distressing circumstances, the future shouldn't seem too promising. So why is there a growing number who view the future with optimism? One reason is because there have been recent successes where people came together and put forth a determined effort to solve such problems. For example, South Korea and Israel have made great strides in reforestation. China has drastically curtailed its population growth. Forty-six nations have agreed on a pact to protect the ozone layer. Environmental disasters from oil spills to radiation leaks, though initially destructive, have had their harmful ecological effects minimized by massive clean-up operations and the restorative powers of nature itself.

Such results have motivated people, even to the point of making great numbers enthusiastic. Those concerned about their own future, and the future of their children and grandchildren, have been stirred to action. The media throughout the world has taken up the cause. Many of the world's largest corporations, long the major contributors to the pollution problem, have renounced their destructive ways and made claims that they have joined the ranks of the solution finders.

NEW AGE SOLUTIONS

In addition to resolving global crisis situations by looking to the latest scientific and technological remedies, a renewed spiritual hope has been proposed. It involves looking to the inner potential of man to solve all his problems and it has become a sweeping movement throughout the world. The basic idea is that mankind has yet to fully tap into its latent non-physical resources — which includes mind and spirit. It is asserted that physical problems can be solved spiritually. And lying within the mind and the spirit, both individual and collective, are incredible powers that are the keys to ushering in a New Age paradise for all humanity.

This has become particularly attractive since most of humanity has been on an unfulfilling materialism binge for nearly a century. By materialism we mean the belief that all things have their basis in physical matter. A strict materialist doesn't believe in things spiritual, including God, angels, spirits, demons, miracles, man's spirit, etc. Since English naturalist Charles Darwin first promoted the origin of life without a supernatural Creator nearly a century and a half ago, the materialistic view has created a tremendous spiritual void. Therefore millions today are trying to fill that mental hollow space. In the process they are turning to the non-material realm for global and personal solutions and there is no shortage of claims, testimonies and hype to slow the trend down.

REPLACING GOD

The impact of one hundred and forty-some years of evolutionary thought has effectively removed from the Western world the belief in God as the personal Creator. It has made great strides toward replacing such a Deity with the deity of humanity, that is, man himself. The claim is that mankind is the highest physical species. Therefore, since we are at the top of the evolutionary ladder, we should look no farther than ourselves for help in solving our problems and controlling our own destiny.

While such an idea may be appealing to many, the fact is, for all the good scientific man has accomplished, he has created more problems than he has solved. The attempts at population control in China, for example, have created other problems. Young couples now limited to one child are, through abortion and the killing of newborn female babies, creating a ratio moving upwards of ten boys to every girl born. Social scientists are fearful as to the impact that will have on future generations. Nuclear energy, to cite another example, has been accompanied by potential radiation dangers as well as the threat of such technology being used to annihilate the earth. The depletion of the protective ozone layer has opened the door for harmful cosmic radiation that threatens to wipe out the human race. Our bodies are being pumped full of molecular time bombs — cancer causing agents — which are the by-products of our latest technology.

Nevertheless, mankind has not given up on itself. It has merely shifted gears to a "higher" level of hope, a hope claimed to be both within humanity and throughout the universe. The basic belief is that man is a part of a greater universal divinity. This un-Biblical divinity is a Great Power or Impersonal Force that exists in everything and can be controlled and manipulated by mankind. This has long been the prevailing view among the Eastern religions, such as Hinduism and Buddhism. And it is now becoming the great hope of the many millions caught up in the New Age movement which is now exploding around the world. It is a belief which rejects materialism, yet still glorifies the potential of the physical side of man. However, man's physical aspect must be in harmony with (some would say in subjection to) his non-physical mind and spirit.

THE BIBLE: GOD'S PLAN UNFOLDED

What we hope to set forth in this book are some perceptions of today's trends as we believe they relate to what the Bible claims shall take place. We cannot address everything but we believe we can show in a simplified, clear and instructive way how currently popular situations, teachings, movements and so forth, can be understood from God's Word. This book takes a Biblical perspective (that is, to the degree that we correctly understand the Bible), because the Bible claims to be God's specific revelation concerning Himself and the nature and destiny of mankind. God, who is infinite and eternal and who alone knows the future, has set forth in His Word the description of events and situations that will take place, and ideas and beliefs that will shape history as it draws to a close.

Here is our premise: Without the insights of the Bible, lots of people may guess but no one can really be sure why things are happening as they are, or what their real impact and future significance will be in the days ahead. Our purpose is to underscore the critical importance of the Scriptures as the only reliable source for understanding the times.

Some of you may never have read the Bible, or maybe only parts of it from time to time. So we offer some basic teachings and a very basic order of events. The content of this book, we pray, will be for all a series of signposts pointing directly to the Bible itself as our only totally reliable source of information concerning the purpose, life and future of mankind.

THE BIBLE: THE ABUSED AND UNDERUSED BESTSELLER

It is a fact that the Bible is the best selling book in all history. Yet given its moral content and then considering the state of the world, it has to rank as the most ignored book in all history.

Although that seems contradictory, there are a number of reasons why such is the case. First of all, though it offers salvation, guidance, and many other wonderful things to mankind, the picture it portrays of humanity is not exactly ego building. Its view of the heart of man is convicting and deadly accurate. So it has become a home decorative item or a once in awhile reference manual tucked away in some corner, but certainly not something of a mirror that one might check him or herself against on a daily basis. The content of the Bible does not lend itself to making the heart grow fond of itself. So it is not the favorite reading of those who work at maintaining a high self-image.

Brilliant men throughout history have sought ways to prove the Bible erroneous — many of whom were subsequently converted by it. Nations, even religions, have sought to stamp it out or restrict its use. That, in a number of instances, however, has ironically led to its most productive use. Yet, the most effective ploy in undermining the Bible has been to make it readily available, give it qualified praise for some of its moral teachings, and promote the rest of it as contrived myths of men. That is certainly the case in the most prosperous countries of the West.

To the evolutionist, the first words of the Bible indicate its mythological nature: "In the beginning God created...." To the materialist scientist, its miracles, from the parting of the Red Sea to Jesus walking on water, make it ludicrous. To the psychotherapist, the Biblical perspective that man has a sin nature is counterproductive to psychology's claim that man can solve his own problems. And to today's educator, it has some literary value as long as its "narrow-minded" authoritarian claims are not taken seriously.

While none of the above criticisms of the Bible has any weight of fact behind it, nevertheless, human ideas and speculations have generated doubts and an overwhelming bias against God's Word. That bias has not only infected the Western world in general, it has, as we shall see, diseased much of Christianity which claims to be "Bible believing."

In the beginning of the Bible we find the first attempt to undermine God's Word. It comes from the mouth of Satan, God's adversary, who deceptively tries to sow doubt in what God has said to Adam and Eve. Satan's first words recorded in the Bible are: "Has God indeed said...?" (Genesis 3:1). The question was followed by enticements based on man's alleged potential to become a god. The consequence was disobedience to God's Word and the result has been a devastated humanity, the minds of which Satan has successfully blinded throughout the ages (2 Corinthians 4:4).

Satan's first scheme has become the backbone of his continuous ploy against mankind throughout the ages. His program is amazingly simple: Undermine God's revealed Word to man and he is left with no trustworthy basis for knowing his Creator, his condition or his purpose. That leaves mankind with only its own ideas and the deceit of the Adversary, whose goal it is to lead humanity down the same path of destruction upon which he himself has been traveling. Satan wants ultimately to bring as many people as he can into the final condemnation which is his destiny: eternal damnation (1 Peter 5:8; Matthew 26:41).

The Bible claims that it is not God's will that any should perish and that He has the way and the means for all those who would turn to Him to live life as it was meant to be lived. Jesus said, "I have come that they may have life, and that they may have it more abundantly. I am the good shepherd. The good shepherd gives His life for the sheep" (John 10:10,11). God wants to protect us from that which brings about destruction. He wants us to know what lies ahead in time and eternity. In the pages ahead we are going to explore what God has set forth in His Word.

2

Some Things We Can't Figure Out On Our Own

There is a theory that is very popular in academic circles, especially in the fields of anthropology, psychology and sociology. It says that God is merely the "creation" of the mind of man. God and the gods are simply the product of fertile imaginations of different people the world over. In other words, God doesn't really exist; men made up the idea. The theory is not exactly scientific, revealing a major bias. Those promoting it are committed to the belief that there is no God higher than man.

The truth of the matter is: Creation exhibits an overwhelming amount of evidence for all of mankind to conclude that a Being of infinitely superior power and intelligence must exist. The complex order of the universe alone should make such an observation inescapable. The book of Romans tells us that all men are without excuse for failing to recognize the obvious in nature (Romans 1:19, 20).

While there are many who do make up their own ideas "about" God, the perspective that "God is a total myth conjured up in man's imagination" is impossible. For if God has no basis other than the imagination of mankind, where did men get the idea of God in the first place? After all, God by definition must be infinitely superior to man. It's impossible to conceptualize something that has absolutely no basis in reality. For example, you can think of all kinds of colors that are variations of the primary colors red, yellow and blue, but try to think of another primary color.

FROM SIN TO CONFUSION

From the time mankind first turned from God in disobedience, right up until this very day, man has taken the belief in his Creator and made the most of altering the details about Him according to his own self-serving reasonings and speculations. "Professing to be wise, they became fools, and changed the glory of the incorruptible God into an image made like corruptible man -- and birds and four-footed beasts and creeping things"(Romans 1:22,23).

The practical problem with such an approach to God is that if He is indeed incredibly superior to man, then man doesn't have the capacity to fully comprehend His character and attributes. "Oh, the depth of the riches both of the wisdom and knowledge of God! How unsearchable are His judgments and His ways past finding out!" (Romans 11:33). It takes an infinite Being to truly know a God who is limitless. "Great is our Lord, and mighty in power; His understanding is infinite "(Psalm 147:5). Any attempt then by man alone to figure out God is at best, folly, and at worst, rebellion. The apostle Paul points out that though men knew God, they suppressed the truth and turned it into a lie. They did not glorify Him as God and became deluded in their thoughts resulting in "their foolish hearts [being] darkened" (Romans 1:21).

While we can never fully comprehend God, God can and does communicate things about Himself that we do have the capacity to understand. If He is indeed our Creator, He ought to know our condition and the limitations of our comprehension and work with us accordingly.

THE BIBLE TELLS US SO

The Bible claims to be the primary means God has chosen to reveal Himself to mankind (Isaiah 8:20). In it are specific things about God that we cannot know about Him except through His telling us. The Bible is, for the most part, the revelation of His personal character, and explains what He is truly like.

God gave us His Word that we might know the truth about Him. It claims to be autobiographical (John 5:39), in addition to its other traits. God is the author; the writers of the Bible over the ages were merely the human vessels through whom He communicated His words. "All Scripture is given by inspiration of God," Paul writes (2 Timothy 3:16). Peter tells us that when God spoke regarding the Scriptures the words were not of any individual's private interpretation, but such "men of God spoke as they were moved by the Holy Spirit" (2 Peter 1:21).

The Bible, therefore, is filled with accurate descriptions regarding the character and qualities of the Creator. Throughout the Psalms His personal virtues are extolled: His lovingkindness, His tender mercies, His faithfulness, His righteousness, His truthfulness, His justice, His generosity, His compassion and forgiveness, His graciousness, His longsuffering, His comfort, and His Goodness.

The Psalmist declares, "Oh, taste and see that the Lord is good; blessed is the man who trusts in Him!" (34:8), and "The Lord is righteous in all His ways, gracious in all His works" (145:17).

Descriptive language abounds from Genesis to Revelation giving us the sense of how God wants to be personally involved in our lives. Psalm 91 tells us that God wants to treat us as a mother bird treats her chicks, covering them with her feathers and hiding them under her wings to protect them from the hunter. In Psalm 23 God's character is likened to a shepherd personally involved in the tender care of his sheep.

The Bible, over and over throughout its pages, tells us what God wants us to know about Himself and what He has in mind for us. Again the Psalmist writes, "You will show me the path of life; in Your presence is fullness of joy"; "I will instruct you and teach you in the way you should go; I will guide you ..." (16:11; 32:8).

We are told that God created us for Himself and that our purpose is to glorify Him (Proverbs 16:4; Revelation 4:11). At first thought that may seem a bit self-serving, not exactly God-like. Perhaps that is because, even though we live in a "what's-in-it-for-me" age, we are still able to recognize the problem of selfishness. But God is absolutely good, "...there is no unrighteousness in Him" (Psalm 92:15). Selfishness is strictly a problem of a sinful nature ...which brings us to what God has to say about us.

MINDFUL OF MAN

The book of Genesis informs us that we are made in the image of God. Though many who promote the idea of man's "infinite potential" are making the most of that idea today, it should be apparent that being made in God's image falls a great deal short of having His divine attributes. People don't create universes. People are not eternal, infinite, unchanging, or omnipresent. God holds all things together. People don't. God is not part of the created universe. People are.

It is our personal qualities that reflect God's image. Only human beings and angels were created in His image. It is man's capacity for morality, love, justice, mercy, intelligent communication, and personal relationship that separates us from the rest of created life. The Bible tells us that these qualities were perfect when God formed Adam and Eve.

SIN CHANGED THINGS

Our original state of perfection, however, only lasted until the first human sinned by disobeying God. Consequently, our image has undergone a great deal of distortion. When you think of a reflected image, usually a mirror comes to mind. A mirror, as we know, is designed to accurately reflect an image of something other than itself. Yet when the mirror becomes warped the reflection is distorted, even though the object it is to reflect hasn't changed.

Sin warped mankind, the "earthen vessel" God created in His image. Therefore, trying to figure out God, who is perfect, by looking at sinful man is like suggesting you can figure out a ceramic artist from a chipped, deformed and crumbling piece of pottery. Certainly there might be some ideas gained from scrutinizing the artifact, but even the best of insights would not be enough to accurately describe the potter. Understanding this concept is crucial to not making God so "human" that we begin to read what amounts to human sinfulness into His personal character. To not be wary of such humanizing opens us up to misinformation regarding the perfect character of God.

KNOWING THE "REAL" ME

In addition to giving us insights into His own character, God reveals to us in His Word what we are truly like. Knowing ourselves, though not as impossible as trying to comprehend an infinite God, is still far beyond man's capabilities. There are a number of reasons why this is so. One is that the Bible tells us that our make-up consists of body, soul and spirit (1 Thessalonians 5:23). While man has a growing knowledge of his physical nature, his understanding of soul and spirit is based upon unprovable reasonings and speculations.

We are not machines that can be governed solely by laws of physics and chemistry. The soul and spirit, unlike the body, are not subject to scientific scrutiny. The epistle to the Hebrews

(4:12) indicates that only God's Word can speak with authority regarding the non-physical side of man. It is a true "discerner of the thoughts and intents of the heart" which have to do with the immaterial aspect of human beings.

Man's sin nature is another reason why we cannot truly know ourselves. The sin of Adam and Eve affected their offspring, the entire human race. "... just as through one man sin entered the world, and death through sin, and thus death spread to all men, because all sinned" (Romans 5:12). Man has borne within himself a heart which the Bible describes as "deceitful above all things, and desperately wicked; who can know it?" (Jeremiah 17:9). Out of such a nature seeps a selfish bias which acts like a filmy covering, blinding our eyes to what we are really like. But God answers the question He himself poses in Jeremiah, "I the Lord, search the heart, I test the mind..." (17:10). In the book of Second Chronicles the writer states, "...deal with each man according to all he does, since you know his heart (for you alone know the hearts of men)..." (6:30 NIV).

THE LIGHT AT THE END OF THE TUNNEL

We think it's more than reasonable to conclude that if mankind has no specific information from outside itself, it is in serious trouble. Without the revelation of the Creator Himself, our situation is akin to a derelict groping about for survival in a dark sewer just before a flash flood. But God has not left His creation to its own futility and destruction.

Our Creator has indeed communicated to us, through His Scriptures, the things that are beyond our capacity to discover about Himself. And they are things He most assuredly wants us to know: "But let him who glories glory in this, that he understands and knows Me..." (Jeremiah 9:24). God has also communicated to us truths about ourselves, our origin, His plan for mankind, and the destiny of His creation, which we will consider in the pages ahead.

3

Past, Present and Future From God's Perspective

In the book of Ecclesiastes we are told that "no one can find out the work that God does from beginning to end" (3:11). God has revealed to us things about Himself and ourselves that are beyond our finding out. He has also disclosed events in the Bible such as man's origin and his final destinations (heaven or hell), as well as significant events in between. Without His divine revelation of these things we could never really know our past, our understanding of today would be superficial, at best, and future events would be nothing more than situations we bump or fall or guess our way into. Without God's light we are doomed to darkness. "Your [God's] word is a lamp to my feet and a light to my path" (Psalm 119:105).

God's essential purpose in declaring what has been known to Him from eternity, that is, what He wants us to know of the past, present and future, is to demonstrate that He alone is God. "Who has declared this from ancient time? Who has told it from that time? Have not I, the Lord? And there is no other God besides Me, a just God and a Savior. There is none besides Me. Look to Me, and be saved, all you ends of the earth! For I am God, and there is no other" (Isaiah 45:21-22). It also demonstrates that He has been, is, and will continue to be, involved in the affairs of mankind throughout its existence. "The secret of the Lord is with those who fear Him, and He will show them His covenant" (Psalm 25:14).

God desires for us to be obedient to His ways. He wants us to be aware that He alone is in charge. " . . .I am God, and there is none like Me, declaring the end from the beginning, and from ancient times things that are not yet done, saying, 'My counsel shall stand, and I will do all My pleasure'" (Isaiah 46:9,10).

Though one can never fathom the depths of God's thoughts about man, He has revealed to us His basic intention. God created us for Himself and for His glory. He created us that we might share in His love and goodness. The Bible contains the record of God's relationship with humanity, and the principle component of His involvement with us is His enduring love.

LOVE INVOLVES A CHOICE

Jesus said that the first and greatest commandment is that we are to love God with all our heart, with all our soul, with all our mind, and with all our strength. Yet to attempt to force anyone to love or receive love would destroy love in the process. Therefore, the necessary condition for love is the freedom of choice. Loving God and being the recipient of His love can only take place in an atmosphere where free will exists.

From the beginning man has had the option to choose God and walk in obedience to His loving ways, or to reject God's way and His love, thus subjecting himself to the destruction that follows disobedience. God could have programmed us to obey Him in all things. While that would eliminate the risk, it also eliminates choice. And without the ability to decide whether or not to obey God, mankind would have been nothing more than programmed robots.

The ability to choose has brought about both the greatest good and the greatest evil. Obeying the will of God is the basis of every true blessing and pleasure that man can receive. And rejecting God's way has been the source of every sorrow humanity ever has or will experience. Throughout history God has poured out His blessings and His judgments upon mankind for the purpose of revealing not only love for us but His justice.

Since the world has been and is comprised of many who have rebelled against God's ways, the punishment at times has been catastrophic. Such judgments have deterred later generations from the same willful rebellion, which also brings its own self-destruction in addition to God's wrath. God does not major in punishment. "'As I live,' says the Lord God, 'I have no pleasure in the death of the wicked, but that the wicked turn from his way and live. Turn, turn from your evil ways!'" (Ezekiel 33:11). The Biblical record tells us of His continuing mercies and longsuffering toward us. Peter writes that God is "not willing that any should perish but that all should come to repentance" (2 Peter 3:9).

LOVE AND SALVATION

It is an act of God's love then that He both inform and warn us of the events which are to take place. It is particularly a measure of His grace and mercy that He tells us of the consequences which stem from man's rebellion, and which can be avoided by those who heed his warning and turn to Him in obedience.

God told Noah what was about to take place because of the wickedness of man throughout the earth. Noah not only preached repentance, but his act of obedience in building the strange and massive ark must have been quite a witness to those who heard his warnings. Noah and his family heeded God's words and avoided the judgment that came. They were used of God to fulfill His loving purposes for the generations to come, most particularly the preparation of a people to receive His Son, the Savior of the world (Genesis 6-9).

God wants us to know what His eternal purposes for mankind are. Not only do such insights offer us hope, especially when we enter times that try men's souls, but our faith and confidence in Him are strengthened when we see evidence of His Word having come or coming to pass.

Since it is the purpose of this book to help its readers better understand the times from a Biblical perspective, we believe it will be helpful to present a synopsis of many of the chronological events given in the Scriptures from Genesis to Revelation that reveal God's plan for man.

GOD'S PERSPECTIVE: PAST, PRESENT AND FUTURE IN BRIEF REVIEW.

In the beginning God created the universe. He created all living things, including mankind. Life appeared suddenly; it did not evolve over billions of years. It was a perfect environment in which plants and animals reproduced after their own kind and flourished. Man and the animals lived harmoniously in a garden environment until sin entered (Genesis 1 and 2).

THE FALL

Adam and Eve, the first humans, disobeyed God. That single act corrupted their nature, the world they lived in, and separated them from God. Through the consequence of their sin, physical and spiritual death entered the universe (Genesis 3).

Adam and Eve were deceived into disobeying God by Satan, a fallen angelic being who had previously led a multitude of the angels into rebellion (Revelation 12:9). God has allowed, for a time, Satan and his demons to be the tempters of mankind (2 Corinthians 11:3,13-15). Since the Fall, the earth has become a battleground for the souls of mankind.

God promised, immediately following Adam and Eve's sin, that He would provide a way for mankind to be reconciled to Him. Nevertheless, mankind would be caught in a constant struggle between choosing God's way or the rebellious ways of sin, self and Satan (Genesis 3).

Ultimate reconciliation would come through the physical sacrifice of God's Son. God's justice required the death penalty be paid by the sacrifice of a sinless man, one not under the death penalty that sin brought about (Leviticus 22:21). Only God becoming a man and offering Himself for mankind would satisfy the requirements of a perfectly just Creator (Hebrews 10:11,12,14).

Animal sacrifices (Genesis 4:4; 8:20) were therefore instituted as a symbol to remind men that they were to look to God for the ultimate and only sacrifice that could save man from his due penalty (Isaiah 53:4-7). Unlike some pagan religions in which sacrificing animals (and people) is supposed to satisfy a bloodthirsty deity, the animal sacrifices commanded in God's law have no such function. Their purpose was to point to the one life, God's only begotten Son, who was to be sacrificed on the cross at Calvary (John 1:29).

Trusting in God for His way of salvation then became the saving faith for every human being throughout history. It also was and is the means of obtaining grace to live lives in obedience to God. Nevertheless, most refused God's provision for salvation and wickedness spread throughout the earth.

THE FLOOD

God judged unrepentant mankind through a worldwide flood, saving only the faithful Noah, his family, and those creatures from which He chose to replenish the earth.

Following the Flood, the generations of Noah's sons worked in disobedience to God's commands, centralizing rather than spreading throughout the earth. They resisted God's purpose for them to replenish the whole earth and came up with a plan of their own. Joining together in rebellion, they built a city and the Tower of Babel as a monument to their pride and resistance to God. At this point all peoples spoke one language.

God, however, intervened. He halted their work by miraculously changing the language of different groups of people. No longer did they remain united in rebellion, and God caused them to be dispersed throughout the earth.

THE CHOSEN

From the family line of Noah's son Shem, God chose a people for a special purpose, the descendents of Abraham. These people were the Jews — whom God prepared to receive His Messiah, the Anointed One He would send to be the Savior of mankind.

God also prepared a land for his chosen people to reside in, and used Moses to lead them and instruct them in His laws. The Jews were to be separate and distinct from the other nations of the earth, serving the one true God.

God chose David, a man after His own heart, who was humble and obedient, to govern the people in God's ways. From the family line of David would come Jesus, the Messiah.

THE SAVIOR

Nearly two thousand years ago, God became a man in the form of Jesus Christ, the promised Messiah, the Savior of the world. He was born of a virgin in Bethlehem of Judah as the prophet foretold (Micah 5:2). This perfect, only begotten Son of God lived a sinless life on the earth. His public proclamation of who He was lasted only three years.

God foreknew that His people would reject their Savior by crucifying Him. The sacrificial death of Jesus, the sinless God-Man, for the purpose of paying the penalty required of every sinner, satisfied eternal justice. Jesus willingly died on the cross, as the perfect sacrifice for our sin, was buried, and resurrected from the dead on the third day. Jesus, in His resurrected body, ascended into heaven where He is today (Acts 1:11).

All who believed and trusted in God for that salvation provision prior to Christ's death, and all who have or will trust Him henceforth, are reconciled to Him and shall be with Him for all eternity. Those who do not believe and reject Christ as their Savior are condemned to pay the penalty for their own sin, which is everlasting torment in the lake of fire, eternally separated from God (Revelation 20:15).

Nearly eight hundred years before Jesus was born in Israel, the prophet Isaiah was told by God that the Jewish leadership would reject Jesus as their Messiah (Isaiah 53:3; Acts 4:8-12). Hosea and Isaiah were told that Jesus would be accepted by the non-Jewish peoples throughout the world (Romans 9:25,26; Isaiah 49:6).

THE CHURCH

After the crucifixion and resurrection of Jesus there began the time in God's predicted plan of events called the Church era. The Church, also referred to in the Scriptures as the Bride of Christ, consists of all those who have put their faith in Christ since His resurrection.

The Church age will end with Christ returning for all those who trust in Him. At some point in history they will be instantly taken up to meet Him in the air in a miraculous event which has been called the Rapture (1 Thessalonians 4:14-18; 1 Corinthians 15:51-53). Later they will return with Christ from heaven after the time of God's wrath upon the earth has occurred.

Following the Rapture of the Church, God's purposes in history will center once again upon Israel, which He promised to restore to their homeland (Romans 11:11,25). The Jewish people will be brought back to Israel after being dispersed throughout the earth for nearly nineteen hundred years (Ezekiel 28:25,26).

The end of the Church age will be marked by increasing activities and movements, those both openly anti-Christian and seductively destructive within Christianity. The Bible refers to this as the Apostasy (2 Thessalonians 2:3).

THE ANTICHRIST AND THE GREAT TRIBULATION

The increase of rebellion at the end of the Church era will prepare the world for the predicted events to come: the rise of a world ruler the Bible calls the Antichrist and the seven year span of his reign known as the Tribulation (Daniel 11:36-39; 12:1).

The Antichrist will take charge of the world's leadership through the power and guidance of Satan, and the assistance of a religious leader the Bible calls the False Prophet. The Antichrist will gain total political, military, economic and religious control over the entire world (2 Thessalonians 2:3-10; Revelation 13).

The Antichrist will deceive Israel, end its restored worship and set himself up to be worshiped by the whole earth. He will force universal submission to his claimed deity through the absolute control of buying and selling. Nearly all those who refuse to worship him and reject his right to purchase mark will be martyred. Those who submit, receiving the Antichrist's mark, will suffer God's wrath (Revelation 13:8; 12:11; 13:7; 14:9-11).

At the midpoint of the seven years of rebellion, God will begin to pour out His wrath against the Antichrist and his worldwide followers. This judgment of God, called the Great Tribulation, will be the most catastrophic event mankind has ever experienced (Matthew 24:15,21,22).

ARMAGEDDON AND THE SECOND COMING

At the end of the Great Tribulation Christ will intervene, conquering the armies of the nations gathered to destroy Israel (Revelation 16:14-16). The Lord will draw all His enemies to the plain of Megiddo in Israel and supernaturally pour out His wrath upon them. This is referred to as the great battle of Armageddon. Jesus, at His second coming, will bring with Him all the faithful who have previously died, or were raptured, or martyred for their faith during the Great Tribulation. They will reign with Him during the Millenium, the thousand year period in which Christ will physically reside upon the earth (Revelation 20:4-6).

The intervention by Jesus will save Israel and the world from total annihilation. He will destroy all those who sought to destroy Israel and preserve the Jewish remnant which remained faithful to God (Revelation 2:25-27; 19:11-21).

THE MILLENIUM

Jesus Christ, the Prince of Peace, will rule over all the nations of the world. From the godly remnant who survive the Great Tribulation will come those who repopulate the earth during the Messiah's Millenial reign. Those who came with Jesus at His second coming shall reign with Him during the thousand year period (Revelation 20:6).

The Antichrist and the False Prophet will be cast alive into the lake of fire, a place of eternal torment. Satan will be bound during this thousand years of worldwide peace and restoration (Revelation 19:19,20; 20:1-3).

At the end of the Millenium, Satan will be released and deceive those born during the 1000 years who have never truly accepted Jesus Christ as their Lord and God (Revelation 20:3,7-9).

Those who join Satan's rebellion, which will end abruptly in a failed attempt to destroy Jerusalem, will be destroyed by God. Satan is then cast into the lake of fire (Revelation 19:20; 20:10).

THE FINAL JUDGMENT

Following the Millenium, all those throughout history who have rejected Jesus Christ will be judged for their sins, justly condemned and cast into the lake of fire (Revelation 20:15). There is no such judgment for those who have received salvation through Jesus Christ. Their salvation was based on His sacrifice on the cross, not their works. However, the good works that they do will be judged and rewarded by the Lord Himself (1 Corinthians 3:14; 4:5; 2 Corinthians 5:10; Revelation 22:12).

THE NEW CREATION

This present creation will be destroyed and God will create a new heaven and earth which shall be free of the effects of sin — no tears, no death, no sorrow, no pain, and no suffering. Only the joy of the Lord. It will be the ultimate paradise in which sin will never enter. Those who at any time in history have placed their faith and trust in Christ as their Savior will live with Him forever (Revelation 21 and 22).

We believe that while the above is no more than a synopsis, it is true to the Biblical record and consistent with the general view the Church has accepted and professed throughout its history. In the following chapters we will be looking at some of the specific accounts of Biblical history and its future predictions in greater detail.

4

God Wants Us To Know What's Ahead

Prophecy, according to the dictionary, has to do with predicting the future under the influence of divine guidance. That definition is accurate in a general way to what the Bible teaches. Examples abound in Biblical history of God speaking directly to men concerning situations and circumstances which would take place at a later time.

The life of Jacob's son, Joseph, included a number of prophetic visions which related directly to his future. He was shown at an early age that he, though next to the youngest, would rule over his father and brothers. He subsequently became the second most powerful man in Egypt, where his brothers and father came under his authority.

God also gave Joseph understanding of a prophetic vision given to Pharaoh which foretold of a time of great agricultural prosperity. That situation, however, would soon be followed by a time of famine. Joseph used the insight to spare Egypt from disastrous food shortages and to provide for the Hebrews, saving his people from starvation (Genesis 37-50).

The fact that one-fourth of the Bible involves predictive subject matter is a strong indication that God, in certain situations, wants mankind to know what is ahead. Future events were continually made known to men to demonstrate that God was involved with them. In many situations He wanted them to make preparations. Sometimes physically and almost always spiritually, depending on the event that would take place. He also, throughout history, had His prophets warn those in rebellion to return to Him, lest they suffer His judgment.

Biblical prophecy, therefore, is not considered by God to be an obscure or concealed subject for only those few interested scholars. It contains very practical information from Him to which His people are commanded to respond.

THE QUICK, THE CAUTIOUS AND THE COULD-CARE-LESS

The subject of prophecy is both zealously pursued and pointedly avoided by many Christians. Some are intrigued by the possibility of knowing what the future may hold, and are eager to be more informed about what the Bible has to say about the future. Others fear that to place one's hope in or alter one's life due to what may amount to a sincere, yet sincerely wrong speculation, is potentially more trouble than it's worth. There are also those who just plain have no interest in putting forth an effort to understand prophecy, complaining that its language is sometimes ambiguous, and there are too many other mental labors involved.

While overzealousness can be detrimental, fear, apathy and laziness regarding prophecy are the greater evils because they are more akin to disobedience. After all, the Bible does present a great deal of prophetic material for the very purpose of being understood and acted upon. God Himself declares throughout His Scriptures that its content is presented at His command, for our benefit. "Who has declared this from ancient time? Who has told it from that time? Have not I, the Lord? ... Look to Me, and be saved, all you ends of the earth! For I am God, and there is no other" (Isaiah 45:21,22). "And the Lord God of their fathers sent warnings to them by His messengers, rising up early and sending them, because He had compassion on His people..." (2 Chronicles 36:15).

There is no doubt, however, that recorded prophecy raises some problems. On the one hand, if it is misinterpreted or misapplied, the results can be disheartening or mistaken at best, and both physically and spiritually devastating at worst. On the other hand, if we tend to avoid or ignore the prophetic insights given in the Bible, we could similarly be led down a path that will eventually end in our destruction.

The solution to such a dilemma is stated clearly in the Psalms where we are given these encouragements: "Your word is a lamp to my feet and a light to my path" (119:105). "You are my hiding place and my shield; I hope in Your word" (119:114). "My help comes from the Lord, who made heaven and earth. He will not allow your foot to be moved..." (121:2,3). "Blessed are those who keep His testimonies, who seek Him with the whole heart (119:2)."

So, no matter what excuses we may bring forth to rationalize away the value of prophecy, the Biblical bottom line is: we are to diligently seek the full counsel of God's Word and be like David, who had a heart to do all of God's will. "But they mocked the messengers of God, despised His words, and scoffed at His prophets, until the wrath of the Lord arose against His people, till there was no remedy" (2 Chronicles 36:16).

THE WAY OF GRACE

Prophecy is confusing to people in some cases because there may be too many different interpretations around clouding what a particular prophecy actually means. Ideas about how certain prophecies will be accomplished, and when they will take place may also be so plentiful that their actual truth could seem to be forever lost in a churning sea of confusion. Some prophecies are more explicit than others. Some have multiple stages of fulfillment. And some appear to be just plain mind-boggling, particularly regarding a prophecy given so far in advance of its fulfillment that it is very hard to tell whether the language is actually symbolic or literal.

However, before one considers "throwing in the prophetic towel," it is good to be reminded that the Lord did not present prophecies for only the most brilliant puzzle solvers. The Bible tells us that it's not those who have the "wisdom of this world" but it is those believers in God who have a heart for truth and look to Him for wisdom who will understand His prophetic word. Jesus made it even more personal, "No longer do I call you servants, for a servant does not know what his master is doing; but I have called you friends, for all things that I heard from My Father I have made known to you" (John 15:15). So God's grace is the main factor here, just as it is with all things that involve doing what He requires.

In the example of Joseph, given previously, the language of the Pharaoh's dream was symbolic: seven fat cows being eaten by seven gaunt cows and seven good heads of grain devoured by seven thin ones. That obviously perplexed Pharaoh. His counselors may have offered their conflicting guesses but none could satisfactorily explain what the dream meant. Joseph, however, was given understanding by God. He then gave Pharaoh the literal meaning: seven years of plenty will be followed by seven years of severe famine.

Joseph explained to the Egyptian ruler that "God has shown Pharaoh what He is about to do" (Genesis 41:25) and Joseph was put in charge of the preparations to avoid the destructive effects of impending catastrophe. It was God's grace to Joseph that saved Egypt and Israel.

Nowhere in the Bible do we find that those people who did not heed God's Word had failed to do so because they weren't intelligent enough, or because they didn't have the prerequisite courses in Hebrew or Greek or dream interpretation. In all prophetic circumstances God communicates what is necessary in order for those to respond to what He is doing and what He wants them to do. His grace will always be sufficient for the task He wants accomplished. Failure to understand is always a matter of an individual being drawn away from God in rebellion, whether that be apathy, self-interest, or just plain hostility towards the purposes of the Lord.

We believe that when it is the time for a prophecy to be fulfilled it will become so self-evident that understanding the prophecy will not depend on one's mental capacity, but rather one's moral submission. God resists the proud, those who put their confidence in their own intelligence, their own abilities or their own way, but gives grace to the humble, those who lean not on their "own" understanding or way, but look to Him for understanding (Proverbs 3:5-7,34).

Blindness to God's written prophetic Word, then, has its roots in pride and disobedience. The solution to blindness occurs when we submit to the only One who can open our eyes, allowing us to recognize what He has made plain. That God will make such things evident and hold us accountable for recognizing them is a matter of Biblical record. "...Write the vision and make it plain on tablets, that he may run who reads it. For the vision is yet for an appointed time; but at the end it will speak, and it will not lie" (Habakkuk 2:2,3).

WORKING THROUGH CONFUSION

The Bible speaks highly of diligence, especially when it comes to gaining wisdom and searching out truth. Paul encourages us to be diligent in our study and application of the "word of truth" (2 Timothy 2:15). Jesus, on more than one occasion, rebuked his disciples and others for not being able to see what was set forth in the Scriptures concerning Himself (Luke 24:25). We are to seek Him with a heart that wants His truth. That is what opens us to His grace which will enable us to understand the things in His Word which may seem confusing.

Consider the book of Isaiah. Isaiah gave a great many of the Messianic prophecies some seven hundred years before Jesus' birth, death and resurrection. In those intervening years many wrongly pointed to individuals and circumstances as fulfillment to Isaiah's words. Many looked to and followed certain individuals they believed to be the Messiah, the Savior and Deliverer of Israel. Because of the mistakes of some, should the people of God have stopped looking for their promised One?

For the Jews of Jesus' era there was a prevailing Messianic bias that only wanted to see the coming Christ as a political savior who would throw off the Roman yoke of oppression. The people were caught up in a practical concern over their political (the rule of Rome) and economic (taxation) problems and looked eagerly for a Messianic candidate to solve their problems. They found and followed a few who claimed to be Israel's Messiah. And while confusion was certainly a part of the times, it was not the heart of the problem.

A DEEPER PROBLEM

Jesus was aware of the confusion, yet He knew Israel would "miss" His coming for deeper reasons. At the beginning of His public ministry He sat in the synagogue in His home town, Nazareth, where all knew Him from youth, and read a Messianic prophecy from the book of Isaiah. Afterwards He declared: "Today this Scripture is fulfilled in your hearing" (Luke 4:16-30). Jesus was telling them that He was the Messiah about whom Isaiah was speaking. While they marveled at His words, there was some confusion: "Is this not Joseph's son?"

Jesus then added a prophecy of His own. He told them that no prophet is accepted in his own country. And just as Israel missed Elijah and Elisha's specific miraculous blessings (they were received by outsiders — the widow from Sidon, and Naaman, the general from Syria), so too, they would miss His blessings. That was all it took to reveal the true nature of their hearts in the matter. Pride and self-will resulted in their blindness to the Word of God and gave birth to rage as they sought to drag Him off and murder Him.

This same scenario took place in Jerusalem three years later when Jesus' prophecy concerning a prophet not being accepted by his own people was ultimately fulfilled by all of Israel. At that time the Jewish leadership was similarly blinded to the words of the prophets by their own self-serving desires, and they rejected their Savior (John 11:47-53).

WITHOUT EXCUSE

Though God knows in advance what we are going to do, we are still without excuse. Jesus did not excuse those who had not heeded the prophets and failed to recognize His clear-cut fulfillment of their words. He rebuked the Jewish leaders for their blindness to the obvious signs He had been doing among the people: "When you see a cloud rising out of the west, immediately you say, 'A shower is coming'; so it is. And when you see the south wind blow, you say, 'There will be hot weather'; and there is. Hypocrites! You can discern the face of the sky and of the earth, but how is it you do not discern this time?" (Luke 12:54-56).

In Luke 24, Jesus pointed to the Scriptures — Moses and the Prophets — which foretold of His death, burial and resurrection as He explained what had recently taken place to two of His disciples on the road to Emmaus. He chided them, exclaiming that they were "foolish" for being "slow of heart to believe in all that the prophets have spoken!" Notice in both cases that "hypocrites" and "slow of heart" are moral accusations, not intellectual ones. Even His disciples had imposed their own self-serving expectations on "their" Messiah and it left them "blinded," perplexed and depressed.

FRUIT OF ACCEPTING OR REJECTING PROPHECY

The Bible tells us that God wants everyone to be saved. It also tells us that not all will be saved. The reason for the seeming discrepancy is that God gives us a choice in the matter. It's the same with prophecy. We can choose to accept the Word of God and walk in obedience to it, or reject it in favor of what we want to happen. While our choice will not prevent God from accomplishing His purpose, it will, nevertheless, effect our lives for better or worse in relationship to the prophetic situation. "Is it not from the mouth of the Most High that woe and well-being proceed?" (Lamentations 3:38).

The rejection and crucifixion of the Messiah by Israel, which the prophets foretold, brought salvation to all mankind. Jesus was rejected by the nation, yet accepted by a number of individuals. The nation, however, reaped the terrible consequences of its choice forty years later when the Temple and Jerusalem were destroyed and its people dispersed. Yet those of the children of Israel whose eyes were opened, and received the prophesied One who was crucified for their sins, had their lives transformed. They were greatly used of God in spreading the hope of salvation to the rest of the world.

So God wanted His people Israel to know what was ahead and to act in a way that would glorify Him, and be a blessing to themselves and others. Some did, but the majority of the people did not. Various aspects of the times certainly added to the confusion, but as we noted, the source of the problem resided in the heart of man. Nevertheless, God's plan for the ages was not hindered, the Messiah came.

5

God's Prophets Foretold, God Fulfilled

Of all the books used as the foundational basis of the religions of the world, only the Bible makes prophetic accuracy one of the tests of its claims to be the truth. That's an amazing characteristic which sets it apart from all other writings — religious, historical or otherwise.

The prophecy fulfillment test is not a minor one. The Psalmist proclaims regarding all of Scripture: "The entirety of Your word is truth . . ." (119:160). Paul writes in the New Testament: "All Scripture is given by inspiration of God . . ." (2 Timothy 3:16). That being the case, any Biblical prophecies not coming to pass for any reason — chance, human, or even demonic intervention, would immediately reduce the Word of God to the level of fraud.

The Bible was written over a period of 1500 years, by more than forty writers from different places, backgrounds, cultures and education. Over twenty-five percent of its entire sixty-six books is predictive of things that must take place after they were spoken or recorded.

Moses wrote the first five books of the Old Testament around 1400 B.C. The last book of the Old Testament was written about 1000 years later and the New Testament was completed nearly 500 years after that. Many scholars believe the book of Job to be the oldest Biblical writing recorded around 2000 B.C. Men, therefore, have had somewhere between 4000 and 3500 years of the Bible's existence to find prophecies that were untrue or had failed to be fulfilled in the exacting details set forth by Scripture.

Attempting to prove the Bible wrong has been the zealous work of many of God's adversaries throughout history, but no one thus far has been able to make a case for its inaccuracy on the basis of prophecy...or any other aspect, for that matter.

THEY PROPHESIED HIS COMING

The Bible lists over 300 prophecies related to the coming of the Messiah which occurred approximately 2000 years ago. They were all fulfilled in Jesus Christ. The prophecies were specific and included hundreds of details which were beyond human control, most particularly the time and place of the Messiah's birth, and the circumstances of His death and burial. A number of contemporary writers have demonstrated that it would be mathematically impossible for them all to occur in any one person's life by chance. The prophecies were declared by God's prophets, and God fulfilled them through His Messiah.

Moses declared that the coming Messiah would be from the tribe of Judah (Genesis 49:10). The Prophet Micah foretold that He would be born in the city of Bethlehem (Micah 5:2). Isaiah stated that He would be in the family line of Jesse (Isaiah 11:1). Jeremiah told us that the Messiah must come from David, one of Jesse's eight sons (Jeremiah 23:5,6). As you can see, these are not vague or confusing predictions.

David, one thousand years before the birth of Jesus, gave some incredibly specific details in the Psalms concerning His death (Psalm 22). Yet crucifixion was not then known to the Jews as a form of capital punishment and quite likely it was mystifying to and misinterpreted by those of David's age and the following centuries. When the time approached for fulfillment, however, that particular confusion which prevailed for more than nine centuries ought to have been obvious to everyone.

The Romans introduced crucifixion in Israel when they took control of the land in 63 B.C. One of the purposes of their form of execution was to display, for all to see, what happens to someone who breaks their laws. It was an effective deterrent that escaped no one's attention for almost a century prior to Christ's sacrificial death on the cross.

Isaiah predicted that the Messiah would die among "transgressors" (Isaiah 53:12) and David prophesied that His garments would be divided and gambled over (Psalm 22:18). Jesus indeed died among robbers, and Roman soldiers cast lots for His clothes. The prophet Zechariah wrote (500 years before the event) that the Messiah's side would be pierced, and Isaiah foretold that a rich man would bury Him. In order to see whether or not Jesus was dead as He hung on the cross, a Roman soldier pierced Jesus' side with his spear. Once Jesus had died, Joseph, a rich man from Arimathea, laid Jesus' body in his own new tomb.

HE CAME AS FORETOLD

Jesus, the Messiah, came as the prophets of old foretold. It was no secret. Angels declared it to shepherds. Signs in the sky declared it to Gentiles.

The message to the shepherds, who were already confused and frightened, was as clear and simple as one could make it: "For there is born to you this day in the city of David a Savior, who is Christ (Greek for the Hebrew term, Messiah) the Lord." The shepherds went to the city of David (Bethlehem), and found "the Babe lying in a manger" (Luke 2:11,16).

The Gospel of Matthew reports that magi from the East, very possibly Gentile wise men, took great notice of a physical sign in the sky, a unique star. It quite likely caused them to search their own books of antiquity and find the Messianic prophecy by Balaam, the diviner also from the East: "... A Star shall come out of Jacob; a Scepter shall rise out of Israel" (Numbers 24:17). That information, as well as what they were able to glean from the books of the prophets of the Hebrews, led them on a journey to Jerusalem to find the coming "King of the Jews." They found Him and "fell down and worshiped Him" (Matthew 2:2,11).

Simeon was a man whom God told that he would not die until he had seen "the Lord's Christ." The Spirit of God led him to the temple on the day of Jesus' rite of circumcision. He took the baby Jesus in his arms and blessed God saying: "Lord, now You are letting Your servant depart in peace, according to Your word" (Luke 2:25-29).

King Herod, upset by the claim that the Messiah was born, had the chief priests and scribes search the Scriptures to locate the place of His birth. The prophet Micah, he was told, declared the birthplace would be "Bethlehem, in the land of Judah" (Matthew 2:6). Herod was so convinced of the fulfillment of this prophecy that he ordered the death of all the baby boys in the area of Bethlehem in an attempt to kill off the Messiah, thus eliminating the threat to his throne (Matthew 2:16).

FULFILLING THAT WHICH WAS WRITTEN

As was noted earlier, Jesus declared who He was in the synagogue at Nazareth by reading from the book of Isaiah. The prophetic words indicating the work of the Messiah were being brought to pass by Jesus. His public ministry, recorded in the four gospels, was recognized by people throughout Israel and into Syria as great multitudes came and were miraculously healed by Him. Jesus fed the multitudes, calmed the storm, walked on water, cast out demons, healed the blind and raised the dead. As Peter reminded the people on the day of Pentecost: "Men of Israel, hear these words: Jesus of Nazareth, a Man attested by God to you by miracles, wonders, and signs which God did through Him in your midst ... God has made this Jesus, whom you crucified, both Lord and Christ" (Acts 2:22,36).

While a man of the Pharisees named Nicodemus recognized the significance of the signs, that Jesus must be from God, he, like the other Jewish leaders, still had trouble accepting Him as the Messiah (John 3:1,2). When Jesus entered Jerusalem with the people crying out a Messianic praise, "Blessed is the King who comes in the name of the Lord!", some of the Pharisees in the crowd shouted to Him to rebuke His disciples. Jesus replied that "if these should keep silent, the stones would immediately cry out" (Luke 19:39,40). The world was to know that He was the Christ.

Jesus fulfilled all that was written concerning the Messiah's first coming. He rebuked the Jewish leaders for their blindness, self-delusion and willful rebellion: "You search the Scriptures, for in them you think you have eternal life; and these are they which testify of Me. But you are not willing to come to Me that you may have life" (John 5:39,40).

HE CAME ACCORDING TO THE SCRIPTURES

The Scriptures had indeed testified of the specifics of the Messiah's coming. Jesus clearly demonstrated that He was like no other man. Why then weren't the Jews willing to accept Jesus? The major reason was their hearts; they willingly chose not to believe in Him. They only saw what they wanted to see in the Scriptures. They wanted a conquering king who would solve their physical problems, not save them from their sins. Jesus didn't fit their self-serving requirements.

From Moses to Zechariah, the Old Testament abounds with Messianic prophecies which spoke of a singular individual who would come fulfilling very different purposes. Such prophecies could only be reasonably accomplished in separate time periods. There had to be two distinct comings in which God's Anointed One, the Savior of the world, would reside on this earth. For example, the Prophet Isaiah gives quite diverse descriptions regarding the Messiah's advents: first, as God coming as a man, born of a virgin, to pay the death penalty required for the sins of all men (Isaiah 53). Second, He will come as that same resurrected and glorified Christ, a King returning to earth to physically set up His kingdom (Isaiah 9, 11 and 12).

The Psalms also underscore the difference between the Messiah's two separate comings. Psalm 22 spells out in graphic detail the death of the Servant, the sacrificial Lamb of God. In great contrast, Psalms 24, 2, 72, and 110 proclaim a different role: "the King of glory shall come in. ... I have set My King on My holy hill of Zion. ...The Lord strong... and mighty in battle. ... All nations shall serve Him. ... He shall judge among the nations."

Jesus' disciples believed that He was the Messiah, although He had told them on many occasions that He would be condemned by the religious leaders, killed by the Gentiles and rise on the third day, they didn't comprehend what He was saying. Their ingrained perspective of the Messiah was that of a ruling king. That's why they were so utterly devastated when Jesus was turned over to the Romans and crucified. Although in His death Jesus fulfilled exactly what the prophets had foretold, the disciples held fast to a scenario which only applied to the Second Coming.

HE'S COMING AGAIN...ACCORDING TO THE SCRIPTURES

After Jesus made His triumphal entry into Jerusalem, according to that which had been written, He lamented over what would soon happen to the city and the Temple. Terrible destruction would come upon them both. He spoke of the city's history of rejecting and killing the prophets and those sent from God (Luke 19:41; 13:34). He gravely mentioned its unwillingness to receive Him. And then He declared, "See! Your house had left you desolate; for I say to you, you shall see Me no more till you say, 'Blessed is He who comes in the name of the Lord!'" (Luke 13:35).

The disciples must have been truly shaken. After all, they had just entered Jerusalem amid choruses of that very cry by the people. The open praises to God for sending His Messiah, the Son of King David, had to have still been echoing in their minds. Only a short while previous they had even argued over who would sit at His right and left hand in His kingdom (Luke 22:24). Now what could He have meant concerning the destruction of the very city in which He would reign? What did He mean — the city shall see Him no more until His coming? Now was the time of His triumphant coming...or was it?

Some of His disciples, Peter, James, John and Andrew, were probably the most convinced of Jesus' imminent reign, and quite likely the ones most upset by His revelation. Andrew was the first of the twelve apostles to follow Jesus as the Messiah. Peter declared Jesus to be the Christ of God, but rebuked Jesus for instructing them about His pending sufferings and death. James and John even asked for top positions in the Messiah's kingdom. The four of them sought Jesus out privately to ask Him questions that must have trembled from their lips: "Tell us, when will these things be? And what will be the sign of Your coming, and of the end of the age?" (Matthew 24:3).

6

The Signs Of The Second Coming

As Jesus sat with His disciples on the Mount of Olives He knew that the words He had pronounced regarding the destruction of Jerusalem deeply troubled them. The Bible says that earlier, when He approached the city amid the multitudes rejoicing at His entry, He Himself looked upon Jerusalem and wept as He proclaimed: "If you had known, even you, especially in this your day, the things that make for your peace! But now they are hidden from your eyes. For the days will come upon you when your enemies will build an embankment around you, surround you and close you in on every side, and level you, and your children within you, to the ground; and they will not leave in you one stone upon another, because you did not know the time of your visitation" (Luke 19:42-44).

Here was the Messiah weeping over the terrible grief that many would suffer because, though He had come for their sake, "they were not willing" to receive Him. It was the Prince of Peace they would reject, as Isaiah referred to Him. And within forty years their enemy, the Romans under Titus, would level the city and the Temple to the ground. One historian commented that so staggering were the numbers slain (600,000), and the amount led into captivity, and the city so decimated, that it had "no history" for sixty years.

"ANOTHER" COMING?

Jesus also knew that his disciples were just as perplexed by Him saying that the city would see Him "no more until" His coming. The disciples, though the Scriptures foretold it and they were informed many times by Jesus, never understood that He would be rejected as the Messiah. That He would be crucified, die, resurrect on the third day, ascend into heaven and sit at the right hand of the Father, and return again at the end of the age were things they did not take to heart.

The only coming that Jesus' disciples had on their minds was that spoken of by the prophet Zechariah: "Then the Lord will go forth and fight against those nations, as He fights in the day of battle. And in that day His feet will stand on the Mount of Olives. ... And the Lord shall be King over all the earth" (Zechariah 14:3,4,9). That was "their" game plan; He was their Messiah, the time was now, and His coming had arrived.

Therefore the words that Jesus spoke which were contrary to their own scenario greatly troubled them. On other occasions when He mentioned things that didn't fit their perspective, they were afraid to inquire further. But not this time. Now they felt compelled to ask Him about His disturbing revelations: "What will be the sign of Your coming, and of the end of the age?" (Matthew 24:3).

FOR THEM AND FOR US

Jesus answered them. Yet He was certainly aware that His disciples would not live to see His second coming or the end of the age. So why then did He answer their questions? Jesus answered them so that they would "watch" for His return (a very important command which we will deal with in later chapters), and for the sake of that specific generation which would read His words and witness the signs of His return.

As we indicated in earlier chapters, there are those who claim to believe in prophecy yet get very anxious when they see attempts at applying prophecy to a specific time period or event. That's understandable. Many efforts have been made in the past and many have been wrong. Nevertheless, even the most staunch (yet Bible-believing) opponent has to concede that Biblical prophecies were made to be fulfilled. And there has to be some point in time in which they are to be fulfilled. So if signs are indeed given to indicate such a fulfillment, those living at the time ought to be able to recognize them. If not, then prophecy is merely some sort of purposeless charade.

THE DIFFERENCE BETWEEN THEM AND US

The thought might have occurred to some that if Jesus' own disciples were confused over His first coming, why would we be any better off today regarding His second coming? Or maybe some are thinking that if they had been given the opportunity to live when Jesus walked the earth, and had the privilege of sitting at His feet, listening to His teachings, and learning from Him directly, they certainly wouldn't have misunderstood. Actually, the firsthand education or the intelligence of the pupils involved was neither the problem nor the solution.

It is true that the disciples spent three years with Jesus and failed to truly comprehend most of His teachings. They abandoned Him when He was taken off to be crucified. They were distraught over His death, thinking their Messianic hope had been dashed. Jesus even had to rebuke them later for not believing the first eyewitness accounts of His resurrection. They didn't exactly pass His personal course with honors. Yet these same men were later described by Luke as having "turned the world upside down" in their effective witness for Jesus Christ (Acts 17:6). What made the difference?

THE NECESSARY EQUIPPING

Jesus told the disciples at the Last Supper that He was going away and that it would be to their advantage (John 14:1-4). He said He would send the Holy Spirit who would dwell within them, teach them, and empower them to do what He taught them (John 14:16,26; 1 Corinthians 3:16,17). The Spirit of Christ, following Jesus' ascension, transformed their lives. It is that same Spirit which, since that time, indwells every believer in Jesus Christ (Romans 8:9-11). "In Him you also trusted, after you heard the word of truth, the gospel of your salvation; in whom also, having believed, you were sealed with the Holy Spirit of promise, who is the guarantee of our inheritance..." (Ephesians 1:13,14).

Scripture tells us that the Holy Spirit has been given to "guide you into all truth" and "will tell you things to come" (John 16:13). The followers of Christ then are able, by God's grace, to understand the teachings of the Word of God.

GRACE AND DILIGENCE

The disciples did not comprehend that there would be two distinct comings of the Messiah. So they mistook the first coming for the second. While that did not prevent Jesus' first coming, it had a great impact on their lives in terms of unfruitfulness and unnecessary personal grief and suffering. And though they had not yet received the Holy Spirit, Jesus, nevertheless, rebuked them for "being slow of heart" to believe the signs, His teachings, and the Scriptures.

Believers in Christ today should be able to avoid such problems. They have the Holy Spirit available on an indwelling basis. Even though they still have the potential to be "slow of heart" in their resistance to conform to God's will, they also have the Holy Spirit within them to "convict" them of their sin as well as teach them (John 16:8-14). A love for God's Word and a desire to know it and do it are important characteristics that God will honor by supplying the grace needed to understand His teachings. "Be diligent to present yourself approved to God, a worker who does not need to be ashamed, rightly dividing [understanding and applying] the word of truth" (2 Timothy 2:15).

While we have been saying that God makes His prophecies clear to those to whom they are intended, we also want to point out that this may involve a good amount of diligence on their part. Peter wrote that the prophets themselves wrestled over the "manner of time" differing between the distinct purposes of the coming of the Messiah (1 Peter 1:10,11). By simple elimination that would not seem to be a problem for us today. Jesus already came as the sacrificial Lamb of God, so there is only one coming left to consider. Right? Christ the King must now return to rule and reign. But what about His coming for the church at the rapture? Isn't that another coming?

THE SECOND COMING — PART ONE

The "rapture" is an event in which Christ will return for all who are saved to take them to that place in heaven He has prepared for them. Believers in Jesus, the Messiah, from the beginning of mankind until the day of His appearing, will be caught up to meet Him in the air. Those who have previously died will be resurrected from the dead and given physical bodies that will never be subject to corruption. Those living at His coming for His bride, the church, shall also have their bodies instantly transformed into physically perfect bodies and return to heaven with Jesus.

Concerning the "rapture" Paul writes, "Behold, I tell you a mystery: We shall not all sleep [die], but we shall all be changed — in a moment, in the twinkling of an eye... and the dead will be raised incorruptible, and we shall be changed. For this corruptible [body] must put on incorruption, and this mortal [body] must put on immortality" (1 Corinthians 15:51-53). "... God will bring with Him those who sleep [had physically died] in Jesus. ... For the Lord Himself will descend from heaven with a shout, with the voice of an archangel, and with the trumpet of God. And the dead in Christ will rise first. Then we who are alive and remain shall be caught up together with them in the clouds to meet the Lord in the air. And thus we shall always be with the Lord" (1 Thessalonians 4:14,16,17).

The actual term rapture is only found in the Latin Vulgate translation but the meaning of the word is applicable to all English translations. It means a carrying away or being carried away in body or spirit.

THE COMING TO TAKE US AWAY

The "catching away" to be with Christ is a unique event. Paul called it a mystery. It was revealed only to those who lived after the resurrection and ascension of our Lord to heaven. There are no teachings regarding it in the Old Testament because it concerned only those living in the Church era of New Testament times. It was only a mystery in the sense that its teaching, when it began, had no previous exposure in the Bible. However, it was not mysterious in that it could not be clearly understood by those who received the teaching.

Yet, the doctrine of the rapture requires some diligence to comprehend. Similar to the puzzling aspects of the first and second time-separated comings of the Messiah, the rapture is the first of two time-separated comings included in the second coming of Jesus Christ. Simply put, Jesus will return first for all those in history who have died in Christ and all those living who are the saved. At the rapture He will not physically touch down upon the earth. So it is quite different from His second coming in which He will rule and reign on the earth. As the Scripture indicates, we (all those living who have saving faith in Him) "shall be caught up together with them in the clouds to meet the Lord in the air."

This is the "coming" that fulfills the promise that Jesus made to His disciples at the last supper: "In My Father's house are many mansions; if it were not so, I would have told you. I go and prepare a place for you. And if I go and prepare a place for you, I will come again and receive you to Myself; that where I am, there you may be also" (John 14:2,3).

NO SIGN NEEDED

After the rapture, and at the end of a period of seven years referred to as the tribulation, Christ will return ACCOMPANIED BY all who were with Him in heaven. "... He is Lord of lords and King of kings; and those who are with Him are called, chosen and faithful" (Revelation 17:14). He will physically return to earth, His foot touching down first on the Mount of Olives (Zechariah 14:4). At this actual return to earth He will intervene saving Israel and the planet from annihilation (Revelation 19:11; Mark 13:20). This is when He will physically begin His thousand year rule over the entire world (Revelation 20).

There are two points we want to emphasize here. One, the rapture, although many consider it part of the second coming event, does not require the fulfillment of any specific sign. Christ's primary purpose is to remove all from the earth who have thus far been saved. Two, the second coming is for the purpose of Jesus Christ returning physically to the earth to begin His millennial reign, and requires a number of signs to be fulfilled first. We believe that though the rapture is not dependent on any sign, it must precede the return of Christ with His saints to rule and reign by at least seven years, the length of time described in Scripture as the tribulation period.

Therefore, as we begin to see last days signs being fulfilled, we know that His coming for His bride must be that much closer. That possibility brings a rejoicing to heart in remembrance of the words of our Lord: "When you see all these things, know that He is near" (Matthew 24:33).

THE SIGNS OF MESSIAH'S SECOND COMING

The first thing that Jesus said to His disciples regarding His second coming was: "Take heed that no one deceives you" (Matthew 24:4). In the Gospel of Matthew and in many other Scriptures throughout the Bible, the days preceding the Lord's return are characterized by religious deception. Paul writes that just before Jesus comes back there will be a great apostasy, or rejection of the God of the Bible (2 Timothy 4:3).

7

Deceiving The World

Millions who started out with the Biblical teachings will turn to a false view of God. Some may have learned about Jesus and Christianity as children, or as once in awhile (or even avid) church goers, yet they were never truly saved. The gradual change to something contrary to their early basic beliefs may have happened without them ever being conscious of it. Others may have consciously rejected Biblical teachings because they were offensive to their lifestyles, adjustments in morality, or even their pride. Many will change to — or with — an evolving counterfeit Christianity. This false church will continue to regard itself as "Christian." However, it will in fact be anti-Christian.

The deception will be so great that even those who are indeed saved, but whose hearts are not totally committed to God's truth, will be seduced. False religious leaders of the day will promote false teachings and practices. Many will be deceived by counterfeit miracles which will attract the masses. True believers may also be led astray for a time, having a detrimental affect on their relationship with the true and living God. While that does not influence their eternal salvation, which came as a gift from God, it will bring destruction into their lives and ruins their life's work which they originally committed to God's glory.

FALSE MESSIAHS PREPARING THE WAY

According to Jesus' words, the last days will also be marked by false messiahs. Many will claim to be the one to save the world from its increasing problems and bring in a time of peace and prosperity. The true Messiah, the Scriptures tell us, is the only Son born of the living God (John 1:14). He is Prophet, Priest and King, the Almighty God Himself (Isaiah 9:6; Colossians 1:15; 2:9). The counterfeit christs will attempt to deceive the people in all those categories. They will be psychics and cult leaders and major religious leaders. They will be military and political dictators and rulers. And they will condition the world to receive the one the Bible calls the "man of sin," the Antichrist. The apostle John wrote concerning "the last hour" that "the Antichrist is coming, even now many antichrists have come" (1 John 2:18).

WARS, STARVATION, AND OTHER DISASTERS

Jesus said that there would be "Wars and rumors of wars" (Matthew 24:6). The wars prior to His coming may be understood as involving great numbers of people all over the world. In other words, such wars would be obvious to a great multitude at the time because they are somehow either directly or indirectly involved. And there will be wars, the nature of which will affect relatively few numbers. They may take place within a small country. Or there might even be an invasion by one nation against another that has little impact on the rest of the world. One may only "hear" of such wars.

There will also be during this time "famines, pestilences, and earthquakes in various places" (Matthew 24:7). In parts of the world great masses of people will suffer from starvation and disease. The failure of crops and the ability of nations to feed themselves will increase. Catastrophes and disasters will be greater and more evident as the time of the Lord's coming draws near. Some of these will be natural events. Others will be brought about by mankind's abuse of the environment, as well as its attempt to solve the problems it created itself.

PERSECUTION AND LAWLESSNESS

These end times circumstances are described as "the beginning of sorrows" (Matthew 24:8). The sorrows will increase in intensity for all involved. There will be great hostility toward those who are truly committed to the God of the Bible. Persecution will come upon true believers from the false "Christian" church, and from the world that rejects the teachings of the Word of God (Matthew 24:9; Revelation 13:7; 2 Timothy 3:12).

Jesus told His disciples that "lawlessness will abound, and the love of many will grow cold" (Matthew 24:12). Life, that is life other than one's own, will be of value only to the degree that it serves someone's selfish desire or interest. So murder, rape, robbery, drugs and the like will be the means through which humans will satisfy their base desires. The people of this time will be totally consumed in "doing their own thing" (2 Timothy 3:1-9). They will refuse to listen to their own consciences, which God placed within each one of us to recognize the difference between right and wrong. The days will see individuals so focused on themselves and their own wants that true love, which is not self-serving, will be a rare experience even among families.

THE "ME" GENERATION

Paul wrote an epistle to Timothy, a young pastor, and informed him of some of the qualities men would exhibit in the "last days." He said the times would be "perilous" because "men will be lovers of themselves," yet "unloving" and "disobedient to parents." They would be "despisers of good" and "lovers of pleasure rather than lovers of God" (2 Timothy 3:1-4).

The days will increase to such wickedness and events will so anger God that He will begin to pour out His wrath upon the whole earth. Jesus describes the days as "great tribulation" which "has not been since the beginning of the world until this time, nor ever shall be." He adds, "And unless those days were shortened, no flesh would be saved" (Matthew 24:21,22).

NOT THE ONLY SIGNS

The signs that Jesus personally gave, reported in the Gospels, were not the only indications of His coming. The book of Daniel and the book of Revelation supply numerous specific details about figures and events of the last days. So too do nearly all of the Old Testament books of the prophets. All of the writers of the New Testament address some aspects and attitudes regarding Jesus' return.

A CHURCH UNTO ITSELF

John, in the book of Revelation, describes the state of the church in the end times. It is clearly a self-centered church which proclaims, "I am rich, have become wealthy, and have need of nothing" (Revelation 3:17). Its works are viewed by Jesus as of no value to anyone. The relationship this church has with Christ finds Him "standing at the door and knock[ing]," asking to come inside for fellowship (Revelation 3:20). This church is not exactly yearning for His soon coming.

THE ANTICHRIST

The book of Revelation is very specific about another coming, one that will occur just before the Messiah returns. The arrival of the individual we are referring to is the false messiah, the Antichrist. He is a political figure who is empowered by Satan to rule the world. He will gain control of a one world government, giving him military, economic, and religious reign over the entire earth: "And authority was given him over every tribe, tongue, and nation" (Revelation 13:7). In addition to military dominance, the Antichrist will govern everyone's right to buy and sell, giving him a control over people never before known in the history of man.

The Antichrist, also referred to as the "Beast," "the Man of Lawlessness," and the "Son of Destruction," will enforce a persecution of God's people which will surpass the total martyrdom of all history. The Antichrist will make all who dwell on the earth to worship Him. He will deceive the Jews and then set himself in the rebuilt temple in Jerusalem to be worshiped as God. Those who refuse to worship him will be killed. Scripture records the scores of martyrs of the "great tribulation" as being so large that they were "a great multitude which no one could number" (Revelation 7:9).

PEACE, PROSPERITY AND THE DOOR SNAPS SHUT

Jesus described the times just before His coming as being similar to the days of Noah and in the days of Lot, who lived in the city of Sodom (Matthew 24:37-39). Wickedness was widespread (Genesis 13:13; 19:13). Nevertheless, people were carrying on their daily activities without a great deal of concern. "They ate, they drank, they bought, they sold, they planted, they built" (Luke 17:28). There was no major situation that prevented them from doing "business as usual." But on the day that Noah entered the ark, and the door was closed, the greatest disaster in history quickly took place (Genesis 7:13-24). In Lot's situation, once he was taken from the city it was totally destroyed (Genesis 19:24-29). The "last days" prior to the return of Jesus Christ will progress in a similar manner.

THE ATTITUDE PROBLEM

Many Scriptures deal with the prevailing attitudes people will have concerning the coming of Jesus. Though seemingly different, they all have their roots in pride, selfishness and willful rebellion. According to the Bible, many of the ones who would be expected to have an interest in His coming, who call themselves "Christians," have been drawn off by other interests. Many will put earthly accomplishments and goals first (Matthew 22:2-5; Luke 14:16-20). Then there will be scoffers who ridicule the idea saying: "Where is the promise of His coming? For since the fathers fell asleep, all things continue as they were from the beginning of creation" (2 Peter 3:4). And then scoffing will turn to bitterness and murder as brother betrays brother, and children betray their parents in persecutions (Luke 21:16,17).

THE BAD NEWS AND THE GOOD NEWS

The signs that have been presented here are not all the signs given in the Bible. There are hundreds more. But these, and a few others, are the ones we would like to consider in the pages ahead. The reasons the signs that Jesus and others gave are not pleasant is because the first purpose of His second coming is that of judgment. Jesus called these times "the days of vengeance" (Luke 21:22). He will return not as the Sacrificial Lamb and Servant, but as the conquering King who will root out all wickedness and judge those who are in rebellion. The signs are mostly fearful in order to get the attention of those who have not thus far feared Him and come to repentance. It is the last chance for salvation for all who live on the face of the earth (Revelation 9:20,21).

Once His judgment takes place He will physically reside in Jerusalem and rule and reign over a transformed earth. "And in that day it shall be that living waters shall flow from Jerusalem, half of them toward the eastern [Dead] sea and half of them toward the western [Mediterranean] sea .... And the Lord shall be King over all the earth" (Zechariah 14:8,9). That will be the paradise restored which was lost at the beginning of creation (Isaiah 60; 61; 62; Revelation 21:6).

MAYBE SO, BUT....

Is there really enough evidence, based on the signs that Jesus, the prophets, and the New Testament writers gave, to conclude that we are the generation which will see the return of the King of kings and Lord of lords? Or are "things continu[ing] on as they were from the beginning" with only an eyebrow raiser here and there to get a few fanatics excited? Well, we the authors are excited. And in the following chapters we will point you to what we believe is overwhelming evidence to justify for us today, the joyful decree of Jesus: "Now when these things begin to happen, look up and lift up your heads, because your redemption draws near" (Luke 21:28).

8
Things We Would Expect To See

If these are really the days just preceding the return of the Lord Jesus Christ from heaven, then there ought to be some pretty convincing evidence around. If the Bible declares that certain things will take place at the time of the Messiah's coming, and Jesus exhorted the generation of His coming to recognize those signs, then we should be able to decide whether or not we are that generation. And as far as we can tell the Bible gives no additional procedures to complicate its very simple test: WHEN YOU SEE ALL THESE THINGS HAPPENING, KNOW THAT HE IS NEAR, AT THE VERY DOOR (Matthew 24:33).

A MONUMENTAL PROPHECY FULFILLED

When Jesus gave some of the signs that would indicate the time of His return, His teaching came right after His prophecy regarding the destruction of Jerusalem. His prophecy was very specific: "... For there will be great distress in the land and wrath upon this people. And they will fall by the edge of the sword, and be led away captive into all nations. And Jerusalem will be trampled by Gentiles [non-Jews] until the times of the Gentiles are fulfilled" (Luke 21:23-24). It is a fact of history, as we mentioned earlier, that in 70 A.D. the city was unmercifully destroyed by the Romans and the people of Judah were scattered to the far corners of the earth as refugees and slaves.

The Jewish people were displaced from their homeland nearly two thousand years ago. History records the continuous attempts to eliminate them altogether, the most recent being the Holocaust under the Nazis, in which six million Jews were murdered. And in those two statements alone are phenomenal situations that have to be considered. An entire nation of people that has been totally displaced and scattered does not enlarge itself among other countries as a national race. They normally marry into whatever peoples they live among and lose their national identity. The longer the time of alienation and mixing with other peoples, the greater the loss of their own identity. The fact that a dispersed people, continually persecuted for over nineteen hundred years, would not only survive as a cultural, religious and national race but increase by the millions, cannot be considered anything less than miraculous.

PROPHECY IN JEOPARDY

The worldwide dispersion of the Jews then was a potentially ruinous situation regarding the accuracy of Biblical prophecy. Jesus' prophetic teachings concerning His second coming would seem to have been greatly jeopardized because the Jews must be in their land when He returns. Yet He Himself predicted the dispersion. However, He also revealed that Israel must be restored at His return. There would have to be a point in history in which the non-Jews ceased their occupation and control of Palestine and Jerusalem. Jesus stated that the Jews would be in Jerusalem at His coming. "O Jerusalem, Jerusalem ... you shall see Me no more till [that day when] you say, 'Blessed is He who comes in the name of the Lord!'" (Matthew 23:38-39). The prophet Zechariah wrote about the proclamation of the Messiah in regards to the day they would see Him: "And I will pour on the house of David and on the inhabitants of Jerusalem the Spirit of grace and supplication; then they will look on Me whom they have pierced" (Zechariah 12:10).

In the hundreds of years that followed the Roman devastation of Israel and Jerusalem, many who studied prophecy gave up on the literal fulfillment of a "resurrection" of Israel as a nation. Although all of the hundreds of Messianic kingdom prophecies depended on it, nevertheless, it was becoming more and more impossible to even consider. However, on May 14, 1948, the impossible took place. Israel became a nation under Jewish rule. In June of 1967 Jerusalem came under Jewish control. Neither of these incredible facts ever came close to being accomplished since the last century before Christ — two thousand years ago.

GOD'S IN CONTROL

In the book of Ezekiel we find: "Then say to them, 'Thus says the Lord God: "Surely I will take the children of Israel from among the nations, wherever they have gone, and will gather them from every side and bring them into their own land; and I will make them one nation in the land, on the mountains of Israel'" (Ezekiel 37:21,22). Did the 1948 restoration involve the hand of God? The Lord Himself answers for all those who witness its fulfillment: "I will place you in your own land. Then you shall know that I, the Lord, have spoken it and performed it" (Ezekiel 37:14).

The significance of the Jews being in and controlling the land of Israel cannot be overstated. The events leading to the second coming of Christ are all prophetically dependent upon such a situation. Therefore, in looking for evidence that will help us recognize whether or not we are the generation of His coming, we can be assurred that this very necessary indicator is miraculously in place. And not only is it in place, but numerous activities throughout the country are proving to be directly related to Biblical prophecy.

PROPHETIC ISRAEL

This small, relatively young state which has been given a second birth, has become one of the foremost military powers in the world today. In his end time prophecy Micah declares, "Arise and thresh, O daughter of Zion; for I will make your horn iron, and I will make your hooves bronze; you shall beat in pieces many peoples" (Micah 4:13).

From its beginnings in the late forties and early fifties as a near wasteland, the country has blossomed into a leading exporter of flowers, fruit and vegetables for the European marketplace. Ezekiel prophesied: "The desolate land shall be tilled instead of lying desolate in the sight of all who pass by. So they will say, 'This land that was desolate has become like the garden of Eden'" (Ezekiel 36:34,35).

The prophet Jeremiah stated, "In those days the house of Judah shall walk with the house of Israel, and they shall come together out of the land of the north to the land that I have given as an inheritance to your fathers" (Jeremiah 3:18). The masses of Jews who are now leaving the Soviet Union for Israel number in the hundreds of thousands at this writing. This miraculous return has been called the "second Exodus" which is a comparison Jeremiah also makes: "Therefore behold, the days are coming," says the Lord, "that it shall no more be said, 'The Lord lives who brought up the children of Israel from the land of Egypt,' but, 'The Lord lives who brought up the children of Israel from the land of the north and from all the lands where He had driven them'" (Jeremiah 16:14,15).

One only has to be a casual news watcher/reader to know full well that Israel is, and has been since its beginnings as a modern state, a continuous newsmaker in world affairs. Its dominance in the Mid-east, its military encounters with its neighbors, its problems within its borders, as well as ceaseless anti-semitism throughout the world, have all made this tiny country (only a few square miles larger than New Jersey) a major focal point among the nations. The Lord God declared through the prophet Zechariah concerning the latter days: "Behold, I will make Jerusalem a cup of drunkenness to all the surrounding peoples, when they lay siege against Judah and Jerusalem. And it shall happen in that day that I will make Jerusalem a very heavy stone for all peoples" (Zechariah 12:2,3).

Clearly the Jewish nation is in that position today and will continue to be until that day in which the Bible predicts all the nations of the earth will be gathered against Israel to bring about its final destruction. Perhaps the next prophetic event that will increase hostilities and further antagonism toward Israel will be the erection of the Temple on the spot where it last stood in 70 A.D. The Bible declares that the Temple must be functioning prior to the return of the Messiah. The reason that this Jewish Temple may cause an outrage is because on the site upon which many believe it has to be rebuilt, presently stands the Dome of the Rock. It is a place sacred to millions of Moslems who believe it is the location where Abraham was about to sacrifice his son Isaac before God prevented it. The possibility that this Islamic holy place could be peacefully terminated is inconceivable.

On the other hand, there are some scholars who believe that the actual site where the Temple last stood is far enough away from the Dome of the Rock to allow a wall to be constructed between them. If their site calculations are correct the Temple could be reconstructed while maintaining the peace, even reducing tensions. But regardless of how it comes about, the Orthodox Jews have long been making preparations for its immediate functioning of the Temple once it is rebuilt.

THE FIRST THING TO LOOK FOR

Jesus was sitting with His disciples on the Mount of Olives and they were within view of the Temple and the city. It was there He began his instruction regarding the last days signs by saying that just before His return there would be great religious deception. His first statement was a warning: "Take heed that no one deceives you. For many will come in My name, saying, 'I am the Christ,' and will deceive many" (Matthew 24:5). He said that these would be false messiahs, and there would be many of them, and they would lead many astray.

Jesus' simple statement is as substantial in terms of fulfilled prophecy as the establishment of the modern state of Israel. And as thought provoking as that may seem, it can be put to a very elementary test. If this is the time of His second coming, then there ought to be many false christs about and they should be deceiving many.

Therefore, consider this. The past couple of decades have seen hundreds, even thousands, coming forth actually claiming to be the Christ. Previous to our generation such a claim was rare. Sometimes hated rulers were labeled as Antichrists. Heroic individuals and liberators were occasionally looked upon by the hopeful as Messiahs. Cult leaders, especially those in the nineteen hundreds who promised paradise on earth, were esteemed as christ figures by their followers and antichrists by their detractors. Add those in insane asylums suffering from messianic delusions and you still are not talking great numbers. At least not enough to promote the situation as a fulfillment of prophecy.

AN IDEA WHOSE TIME HAS COME

Many may not be aware that newsworthy figures such as cult leaders Jim Jones, Charles Manson and Sun Myung Moon, TM founder Maharishi Mahesh Yogi, and a number of internationally influential Eastern gurus including Sai Baba, and recently deceased gurus such as Muktananda and Bhagwan Rajneesh, have all made "christ" claims concerning themselves. Their hundreds and, in some cases, millions of followers are certainly aware of that fact. But you don't have to be in a cult to get the message. Millions the world over who read any major newspaper back in April of 1982 were aroused by a full page ad claiming that the "Christ" is present among us. Literally hundreds of cult leaders throughout the world are promoting themselves as "Christs." Yet that number is minimal compared to the multitude of other "Christs" now coming forth. The primary reason has to do with currently popular twists in who or what exactly is the "Christ."

"THE CHRIST" IS NOT EXCLUSIVELY JESUS

According to the view which is promoted by the Mind Science cults and numerous other occult groups, "the Christ" is not unique to the person of Jesus who lived in Palestine some two thousand years ago. It was a spirit or Spirit that He greatly exhibited in His life. We are told that we all have the potential to be "Christs" just as He (or he), a mere human no different than any of us, reflected.

THE CHRIST CONSCIOUSNESS

"The Christ" is also being pushed as a consciousness or mind experience affecting groups of people. Many coming together utilizing different techniques such as meditation, chanting, and drugs believe they can be "overshadowed" or mystically influenced by a spiritual energy. The experience they have together is said to empower them to manifest "the Christ" as a group.

UNIDENTIFIED FLYING MESSIAHS

UFOs are said to be the only Messianic hope for all mankind according to the ever increasing numbers who claim to have made contact with them. The alleged aliens consistently promote the message that they will save the world from pending destruction and guide humanity into its next phase of evolution.

SPIRIT CHRISTS

The multitudes today (in the millions) around the world who are contacting spirit guides or non-physical entities through spiritists, mediums, and channelers are contacting "spirit Christs." These also include those using Ouija boards, crystals, meditation techniques, attending seances, or taking mind altering drugs. Some of the spirit entities claim to actually be Jesus; most represent themselves as one of multitudes who have manifested the Christ spirit. But all deny the uniqueness of Jesus, whom the Bible says is the only begotten Son of God — God who came in the flesh.

The apostle John, reflecting a concern over the deception that would come about regarding the true Christ, wrote these words of instruction: "...every spirit that does not confess that Jesus Christ has come in the flesh is not of God. And this is the spirit of the Antichrist..." (1 John 4:2,3).

THE HUMANISTIC CHRIST

Many liberal denominations that profess to be Christian, and a growing number of reformed Jewish rabbis, teach that "the Christ" is nothing more than people living up to their inherent goodness and potential, no matter what religion they are involved in. They teach that Jesus was just one of the many throughout history who greatly demonstrated the divinity that resides within us all.

THE REINCARNATION EXPLANATION

The phenomenal influence of Eastern religions in the world today has also added to the fulfillment of Jesus' prophetic warning regarding the rise of many false Christs. Reincarnation is a basic Hindu doctrine that the popular guru missionaries from India have presented to try to show the unity of their teachings with Christianity. Reincarnation, in its Westernized rendition, primarily involves a belief that a human's soul has always and will always exist. The claim is made that the soul simply goes from one body at death to another at conception or birth for its next physical life. This cycle goes on continuously until it evolves to a higher form which has no need of a physical body.

Though the Bible clearly rejects the teaching of reincarnation, scores of thousands of professing Christians are being deceived by such beliefs. The Scriptural perspective is that physical death for a person occurs only once, there are no second, third and so forth chances. "... it is appointed for men to die once, but after this the judgment" (Hebrews 9:27). The Bible teaches that the spirit and soul begin at conception and continue after one's death. There will then come resurrection, when one's spirit and soul will be given a body that will never die, but last forever (1 Corinthians 15:42). Those who have trusted in Jesus Christ as Savior will live with Him throughout eternity. Those who have rejected the person of Jesus Christ and His salvation will pay the penalty for their own sins: everlasting punishment and separation from God (Daniel 12:2).

THE GURU CHRISTS

Through the process of reincarnation, the gurus tell us, the same spirit/soul that occupied the body of Jesus has subsequently entered the body of numerous generations of individuals since the time of Christ. When a soul is of special significance, and will greatly affect the evolution of mankind, it is said to reincarnate as an avatar, a god. Avatars are Hindu versions of Messianic saviors for the human race. Hindus believe that Christ was a reincarnation of their god, Vishnu, and they are looking for him to come again as the avatar, Kalki. At the very least this belief offers a religious rationale for claiming to be the Christ. There are thousands of Indian gurus today who are considered by their millions of disciples to be the Christ reincarnated avatar.

The various false "Christ ideas," while growing and deluding millions around the world, are only a small part of the deception to which Jesus referred to in Matthew chapter 24. As we shall see in the following chapters, the ultimate delusion does not seem to have any boundaries.

9

Delusion And Confusion

The New Age Movement is the largest and fastest growing religious movement in the world today. It involves tens of millions of people. One of its major purposes is to bring a unifying basis to all the religions of the world in order to further universal peace and harmony. It sees differences in religions and religious practices, from witchcraft to the Catholic Church, from Satan worship to Buddhist meditations, from sacred drug rituals to holy communion, as merely superficial expressions or differing paths that all lead to God. It therefore promotes all of the un-Biblical christ perspectives mentioned earlier.

In addition, it aggressively attempts to combine science and religion. One example involves the promotion of the so-called scientific belief of psychology's "collective unconscious," that is, that within mankind there is a deep level of thought of which we are not consciously aware. They believe we are all "connected together" at such a point and this "collective unconscious" has the potential to solve all of our problems and lead us into the next phase of our evolution. It is referred to by proponents as the soul of "Christ consciousness."

RAISING "HIS COMING" CONSCIOUSNESS

In the gospel of Luke, Jesus tells us that the many who come in His name, claiming to be the Christ, will also promote the idea that the time of the end "has drawn near" (21:8). It will be part of the deception He predicted. It seems that one of its purposes is to confuse the actual time of Christ's return with not only false Christs and deluded Messiahs, but with so many views of what His coming is all about that it will perplex and deceive a great number. Some will be led astray, others will point to the confusion and become scoffers. In either instance, they will have turned away from the truth.

RELIGIOUS DECEPTION & THE FALLING AWAY

The first warning "signs" Jesus gave raised a great concern about deception. While He indicated that the focus would involve deceiving people as to the truth of the Messiah Himself, and His coming, it is understood that certain things would have to occur to prepare and set people up for such a delusion. The coming deception would be religious and it would be massive.

Referring to the times of Jesus' return, the apostle Paul echoed Christ's words when he wrote: "Let no one deceive you by any means; for that day will not come unless the falling away comes first..." (2 Thessalonians 2:3). The falling away referred to here has to do with great numbers turning from the truth of Biblical Christianity. These include multitudes who 1) professed to being Christians at some point in their lives but since have become extremely opposed to Christianity; 2) continue to profess to be Christians but deny the basic doctrines of the faith; and 3) those who are indeed Christians, yet have become deluded by and entrenched in false religious beliefs and practices. This last category of Christians are affected to the extent that their lives and works produce no fruitfulness or glory for the Lord. They will also become part of the end times deception by leading others astray.

DEMONIC FUEL FOR THE FIRE

Jesus, in giving the end time indicators to His disciples, issued another grave warning as to how extreme the religious delusion would be: "For false Christs and false prophets will arise and show great signs and wonders..." (Matthew 24:24). These counterfeit miracles would be so convincing that those who truly believed in Jesus might also be deceived to some degree or for a time. Paul, guided by the Holy Spirit, wrote, "Now the Spirit expressly says that in latter times some will depart from the faith, giving heed to deceiving spirits and doctrines of demons..." (1 Timothy 4:1). Paul told the Thessalonians that all these things would be according to the working of Satan who, along with his demons, is the one behind the lying signs and wonders.

APPLYING THE TEST

Are we in or approaching a time of unprecedented religious apostasy and deception, lying signs and wonders, and doctrines of demons? There are a number of books available which have documented such evidence in great detail, so our purpose here is only to present some "tip of the iceberg" examples found throughout Christiandom which we believe certainly qualifies this generation for witnessing the return of Jesus.

THE UN-LIBERAL BOOK

It is a fact that never before in history have there been so many Bibles available. At the same time, the Word of God's influence upon those who profess to be Christian is inconsequential. The "lamp" of a great part of the church is either barely flickering or completely extinguished. Therefore little or no light is available to discern religious deception. Consider the following.

ECUMENISM

Pope John Paul II, the head of over 800 million Catholics, on a recent visit to India, praised the pagan religions of the East (Hinduism, Buddhism, etc.) for their rich spiritual heritage. He stated that because of India's "intuition of the spiritual nature of man ... [her] greatest contribution to the world can be to offer it a spiritual vision of man."[1] Such a "spiritual vision," however, is rooted in pagan spirituality which the Bible, from Genesis to Revelation, condemns as idolatry and spiritual adultery.

The pope invited Christian and pagan religious leaders from around the world to participate in a prayer "Summit for Peace and Brotherhood." The unprecedented spiritual event included American Indian medicine men, African animists, Hindus, Sikhs, Buddhists, Moslems, Shintoists, Jainists and assorted Christian denominations. Each representative was to invoke his own god for world peace.

Robert Runcie, as Archbishop of Canterbury, was head of the Church of England and spiritual god-father to the American Episcopalian Church. Prior to retiring he presided over a world conference on "Religion and Ecology" attended by numerous pagan religious leaders including the Dalai Lama, considered by Tibetan Buddhists to be their god-king. Runcie's replacement, by the way, is George Carey, who claims to be an Evangelical. Nevertheless, he "rejects a literal interpretation of the creation and Adam and Eve in Genesis" according to a *Time,* August 6, 1990 story.

BIBLICAL SCHOLARS?

The last few years have seen so-called "theological think-tank" conferences gaining a great deal of publicity for their pronouncements regarding Jesus and the Bible. Some statements include: 1) Jesus was not celibate. 2) He only actually said a small portion of those things attributed to Him in the Scriptures. 3) He was shiftless and disrespectful. 4) He did not predict His death on the cross. 5) He did not promise, nor did He expect to return to earth and usher in a new kingdom.

THE CHURCH AT SODOM

Many of the mainline Christian denominations are advancing homosexuality as a "lifestyle of choice" rather than an abomination before God. Today, ordination of practicing homosexuals is openly performed and promoted. The Episcopal bishop of Newark, New Jersey, John Spong stated in an article for the July 31, 1988 *Washington Post,* "The time has come for the churches of America not just to tolerate, but to celebrate and welcome, the presence among us of our gay and lesbian fellow human beings."

DOCTRINE DUMPING

A number of prominent church leaders who profess to being Evangelicals are selectively tossing aside critical doctrines as irrelevant. For example, Norman Vincent Peale, pastor and publisher of *Guideposts* magazine, with subscriptions of over 4.5 million, has stated that the virgin birth of Jesus Christ is just "some theological idea" which is of no real significance.[2] However, since the virgin birth fulfills Biblical prophecy, and is necessary for the sinless nature and the deity of Jesus, not to believe in His virgin birth is a rejection of the Biblical Jesus.

EVANGELICAL gODS

Perhaps the most astounding trend in Christianity today is the belief that humans are gods. The teaching is promoted by leaders in the church who are influenced by Eastern religions. Their view is a pantheistic one which claims that God is everything, and we are a part of God; therefore, we are God (though a small part).

The fastest growing movement within Christianity, the Faith or Positive Confession Movement, advances a related idea by saying that man was created as the god of this earth, but has lost that position to Satan and is now in the process of recovering it. The fact that it was Satan himself who originally offered godhood to Eve hasn't phased such "Faith" teachers. Some of its leaders are convinced that the children of God must be gods.[3]

EVANGELICAL TAKE-OVER

While liberal scholars have made claims that the Bible doesn't support the view that Jesus will return to earth to set up His kingdom, many Evangelical leaders are teaching that Jesus cannot return to earth until Christians take control of the world. Through the application of Biblical law and under the direction of Christian leadership, they believe the earth will blossom into a paradise. They teach that the process will cause the lost to see the benefits of God's way and will influence them to receive salvation.

There are quite a few variations on this theme in the church today involving a wide spectrum, from the most extreme Charismatics to the most legal Fundamentalists. Yet for those who hold it, all have a common objective: Christians must take dominion and the physical kingdom of God must be established on earth in order for Christ to return. We will deal with this in greater detail in a later chapter. But what should be apparent in this Christian victory scenario is that it denies almost all of the prophecies regarding what must actually take place just prior to the Lord's second coming.[4]

TEST ALL THINGS

The church, throughout its history, has had its problems with false teachings and teachers. There are many warnings written in the New Testament for the first century church to be on its guard for views and practices that deviated from the teachings they had originally received. The Thessalonians, to whom Paul wrote around 51 A.D., are an example of a people who were deceived and confused by the timing of the Lord's coming.

They were persuaded, both by false teachings and by the persecutions and the tribulations they were experiencing, that they were in the day of the Lord. This had left them greatly disturbed because Paul had written to them that God did not appoint Christians to suffer His wrath during the great tribulation (1 Thessalonians 1:10). In ministering to them by letter, Paul commended them for their patience and faith in enduring the afflictions they were suffering, but repeated the simple instruction he had given to them when he was among them. There were very specific and identifiable things that had to take place prior to that day. If they did not see such events taking place, then it was not the time of His coming.

At the end of his first epistle to the Thessalonians, Paul exhorted them to "Test all things" (5:21). That is further encouraged by Peter, Jude, and John, as they pointed to the latter times to warn of unprecedented religious deception. In the next chapter we will continue discerning the times, events and circumstances to see if they qualify as fulfillments of the signs of the last days before the coming of Jesus Christ, our Lord and Savior.

10

Getting Back To Basics

Sometimes when we are discussing the signs signifying the return of Jesus Christ, it is not uncommon for certain objections to arise. They are usually along the line of, "Yeah, but lots of people thought Hitler was the Antichrist and they all thought Jesus was going to return then." It can be frustrating to be continuously reminded of the many misattempts throughout the centuries to label some period as the time of Jesus' coming. But if such a frustration were to dampen one's enthusiasm for looking for Christ's return, it would be, in our view, a greater error than misreading the signs.

Why is it a greater error? Well, it's not a suggestion but a command of Jesus that we be "watchful" and "look" for His coming. To be put off by one or more objections that sound reasonable can amount to disobedience to His will. We should consider all objections in the light of Scripture. If our understanding of the times does not have Biblical support then we have no true basis for our belief. On the other hand, we are not to be dissuaded by even a flood of disagreements if they themselves have no Biblical basis. We have to remember that it is God's Word that warns us that we are not in darkness that the day of His coming should overtake us as a thief in the night. In other words, He has provided enough "light" for those in the time of His coming to recognize it with assurance. But it is up to us to make sure that we are in line with Scripture so that we can be truly discerning and not caught unaware.

With regard to those who point to all the miscalculations and misapplications of the past, such errors are not to be the basis for not being obedient to the command to continue to look for Jesus' coming. We ought not let mistakes of the past pressure us away from doing what is right. And regarding such past misapplications of prophecy, all efforts at claiming earlier centuries of history as the time of His coming had missed a major sign: the restoration of Israel. No matter what sign seemed so sure or how "Antichrist" any political figure of an earlier time may seemed to have been, without the Jews back in control of their land, the return of the Messiah could never be fulfilled according to prophecy. On that one count alone, 1948 (the year Israel was restored as a sovereign state) could well be the most significant date thus far in the last days prophetic calendar.

THE POST 1948 DATE SETTING CONFUSION

For a great many who are zealous for the return of Jesus Christ, it is difficult not to become excited over the possibilities of His soon coming now that Israel has been restored. That zealousness, in some cases, however, has given birth to foolishness. More than a few have attempted to accurately calculate the year, even the day and hour of His return. Many of the predicted dates (which were often highly promoted) have come and gone creating serious problems. Great numbers of people were left confused. The effect has been to create a climate of skepticism and even cynicism regarding the coming of Jesus Christ. Such endeavors, no matter how well meaning, are contrary to both the letter and the spirit of what the Bible tells us in consideration of the last days.

The Bible encourages an attitude of great expectation among the faithful concerning Christ's return. It gives instructions about how we should act in anticipation of His appearing. It tells us that we should be like one who is constantly alert to the possibility of

His coming. It gives us the signs surrounding His coming for two primary reasons: One, so that we can know that the time is near and, two, so we can understand the times and know how we should live relative to what is taking place.

The Bible does not give last days signs in order to calculate the exact time of Christ's return. To do so would be contradictory to its numerous exhortations for us to be watchful and vigilant concerning His appearing. If we knew the exact time of someone arriving at the local airport, would we get excited and show up at the gate years, months, weeks, or even days in advance looking for the flight? Of course not. Knowing the exact time virtually eliminates carrying out the Biblical command to have an attitude of continual watchfulness.

We believe that the times we are living in qualify according to the signs Jesus gave in reference to His return. Our belief, whether right or wrong, nevertheless involves submitting to the Biblical mandate by putting forth the effort to find out. That is really the heart of the message of this book. We want to encourage our readers to know and be obedient to the instructions of the Bible with regard to their attitude and actions concerning the times of the Lord's coming. To deviate from its commands, for whatever reasons, is to not only become personally unfruitful, but to contribute to the delusion that characterizes the last days. Date setting, among other un-Biblical practices, has been and continues to add to such delusion.

THE "BASICS" OF THE LAST DAYS SIGNS

Before we go on to consider more signs that Jesus gave regarding His return, we think it's important to be reminded of the chief characteristics of the signs of the last days.

1.) The signs of the last days are given for our instruction so that we can know whether or not we are the generation of Christ's second coming.

2.) The signs Jesus gave are primarily warnings. He began listing the signs by saying, "Take heed that no one deceives you" (Mark 13:5).

3.) The signs indicate that the times preceding His return will be times of conditioning and preparation for the worldwide acceptance of the Antichrist, his kingdom, his rule, and his religion.

4.) The last days "preparation" signs primarily involve religious apostasy and delusion. To neither be aware of the signs nor understand what they are about is to leave oneself wide open to their deceptive characteristics. In addition to avoiding self-deception, each Christian also has the responsibility of witnessing to and rescuing those who have been seduced by the false beliefs, practices and programs that will abound prior to Jesus' return.

5.) Some of the signs have been foretold as a deterrent. We believe that the last days signs are forewarnings of God's judgment to be poured out upon the earth. They are for those who will respond by turning to God to be saved, and thus avoid His wrath which is directed at the rebellious who reject His offer of salvation.

While the above points are important for understanding what will take place prior to Christ's return to rule on earth, we have to keep in mind that the blessed hope of the church, the rapture, has no prophetic signs requirements that must be fulfilled in order for it to occur. The Scriptures indicate that the rapture precedes the second coming of Christ to begin His millennial reign. Therefore, as we see prophetic signs in the process of being fulfilled, we can know that the appearing of our Lord for His bride, the church, is that much closer to taking place. As Jesus Himself stated, "Now when these [signs] begin to happen, look up and lift up your heads, because your redemption draws near" (Luke 21:28).

PREPARATION FOR DELUSION

In a previous chapter we covered two major signs that Jesus gave which we see being fulfilled today: widespread religious apostasy and deception, and the greatly increasing numbers of those coming forth making claims to being the Christ. We believe these to be very significant because they are foundational to making the world ready to accept the false political and religious leader the Bible calls the Antichrist.

As we stated above, the last days before Jesus, the true Messiah, returns to earth will be days of the Antichrist's rule. That Biblical fact is critical for every Christian to understand in order not to be duped into supporting plans or programs that are part of the preparation for the one the Bible also calls the Beast. While we believe (and shall explain in the chapters ahead) that those truly committed to Christ prior to the rapture will not be on the earth during the reign of the Antichrist, they will, however, be subject to the powerful delusion which will begin to indoctrinate the entire world before the rapture. Therefore, knowing what the Scriptures clearly teach about the events of the last days is essential. Without such knowledge many sincere Christians and professing Christian organizations will be seduced into contributing to the Antichrist's coming agenda.

TIMES OF PEACE, PROSPERITY AND SUDDEN DESTRUCTION

Our understanding of the end times Biblical scenario is as follows: At a certain instant in time Christ will appear in the clouds above the earth. He will rapture or catch up to Himself all who have believed in Him, taking them from earth to heaven. Removing all those who are committed to the true Christ will effectively end all resistance to everything that has been preparing the way for the Antichrist.

At that point in time the earth will begin to openly follow the Antichrist, a human being empowered by Satan who will be the ultimate counterfeit of the true Messiah. Previous to the Antichrist's appearance, the entire world will have been conditioned in every area — politically, militarily, economically, sociologically, psychologically and spiritually — to accept this one whom it believes will save it from all its problems and usher in the age of peace and prosperity.

This world ruler, whom the entire earth will also worship, will reign during a seven year period. He will control all commerce. No one will be able to buy or sell without first receiving the Antichrist's qualifying mark. Receiving the mark will also be a religious act of submission. Those not taking the mark will be martyred for their refusal to worship the Antichrist. For the first three and a half years of his reign he will seem to be successful in solving the world's ills, but then circumstances will deteriorate rapidly.

At the midpoint of his reign the Antichrist will commit the ultimate act of blasphemy by setting himself up in the Temple in Jerusalem and declaring himself to be God. Because of this abomination and desecration of the Temple, God will begin to pour out His wrath upon all the earth. For the final three and a half years humanity will suffer the greatest affliction and catastrophies in its history. The Antichrist's reign will end when all nations are gathered together to destroy Israel in the ultimate war the Bible calls Armageddon.

At the height of this final world war Jesus Christ returns from heaven with all those throughout history who have trusted in Him. He will intervene in order to save the planet from total annihilation. The Lord then begins His millennial reign, restoring the earth to the paradise it was at its creation.

It is important to understand that these events are what the last days are all about. To be persuaded away from the clear teachings of the Bible to something that may seem more positive or optimistic is to do so with no basis in truth. Some may not like the above scenario for various reasons. But if those who protest to such a view have reasons other than the claim that they are not accurate to the Scriptures — which each one of us has a personal responsibility to understand and submit to — then those making the complaints have set themselves up for becoming part of the delusion (2 Thessalonians 2:10,11). Without an accurate understanding of the last days, there is little hope to responsibly discern the signs that Jesus gave us.

11

Signs Of The Times

Jesus told his disciples that the times prior to His return would be characterized by "wars and rumors of wars" and by "nation rising against nation" (Matthew 24:6,7). Certainly wars and rumors of wars and nation rising against nation could apply to almost any century since Christ spoke those words. But we believe it is significant that this century has experienced the wars "to end all wars." World Wars I and II have raised awareness among all the peoples of the earth that a third such war would be to no one's advantage. It would most likely bring the kind of widespread destruction to the planet that would leave it beyond repair. That consequence is a major deterrent that no generation previous to this nuclear holocaust conscious age had considered.

It is also interesting to note that the wars following the second world war have been by comparison "rumors of wars." From the United States' conflicts in Korea and Vietnam to the U.S.S.R.'s occupation of Afghanistan, from the Mid-East battles between Israel and the Arabs, between Iran and Iraq, to the brief clash between Great Britain and Argentina, none have come close to the all out conflagration which took place between the major powers of the world. They have been limited in numbers and devoid of the most potent weaponry available, especially nuclear and thermonuclear weapons.

While no person can absolutely predict that a major powers conflict will not take place, those who are regarded as experts in military affairs see the years ahead as involving only "low intensity conflicts." These may include brief confrontations utilizing limited conventional weapons, longer but still limited guerrilla warfare campaigns, and state sponsored international terrorism. Such a trend seems to conform to the idea of "rumors of wars." Even at this writing, the present invasion of Kuwait by Iraq has brought a unity of world military powers against any country who would overtake another country by military force.

After mentioning the wars and rumors of wars, Jesus added that there would then follow a length of time before the end comes (Luke 21:9). If by that He meant a time of world peace, it would not only fit the days in which we are living but underscore such increasingly accepted activities as the international peace movement as evidence. Such a time of peace would also be in agreement with the last days sign Paul gave in Thessalonians: "But concerning the times and the seasons, brethren, you have no need that I should write to you. For you yourselves know perfectly that the day of the Lord so comes as a thief in the night. For when they say, 'Peace and safety!' then sudden destruction comes upon them, as labor pains upon a pregnant woman. And they shall not escape" (1 Thessalonians 5:1-3).

In the gospel of Luke Jesus described the days just prior to His coming as being similar to the day of Lot, a period of peace and prosperity with nothing, particularly war and worldwide cataclysm, going on to disrupt business as usual. "They ate, they drank, they bought, they sold, they planted, they built; but on the day that Lot went out of Sodom it rained fire and brimstone from heaven and destroyed them all. Even so will it be in the day when the Son of Man [Jesus, the Messiah] is revealed" (Luke 17:28-30). The destruction will suddenly break in on a peaceful and materially thriving world.

WORLD PEACE AT LAST?

It certainly seems that this generation is unique in its potential to bring about world peace. The Cold War, with its umbrella of nuclear devastation hanging over us, is being perceived by many today as a once foreboding dark cloud blown away by recent winds of change. The political changes taking place in communist countries, and in the Soviet Union in particular, have given great hope to all but the most cynical. While the changes taking place are mind-boggling, they aren't occurring without cause. There are many things, both old problems and new solutions, which have contributed to this potential fulfillment of prophecy which were not possible in prior times.

Technology, especially the state of the art of communications, has rendered ineffective all barriers to keep foreign information out of even the most totalitarian countries. Such information, graphically presented through the visual media, invites comparison between economies. As great numbers of people recognize that they are severely lacking compared to other countries, they will eventually push for change. World communism, which has had continually increasing economic problems, is undergoing such a development.

WAR AND THE BOTTOM LINE

There was a time when war was profitable. Nations assaulted other nations and looted, plundered, and pillaged, making off with goods, livestock, slaves, entire treasuries, and so forth. Occupying the land for its natural resources and/or taxation purposes must also have been worthwhile. If it were not generally profitable, we don't believe the activity would have endured over the centuries. Man's self-serving nature does not push him to continue unrewarding endeavors.

Today, war doesn't pay. And there is a definite trend away from it. Here are a few of the reasons: Increasing military costs have created even greater burdens upon many national economies, most notably the already severely strained Soviet Union. World domination by military might has more and more come to be recognized as a dictator's insane delusion. The occupation of one country by another has proven to be the invading country's nightmare, both economically and psychologically. Limited conventional warfare at this day's armament rates is prohibitive. No one wins in a nuclear war. And advances in surveilance satellite technology have all but eliminated keeping large military operations secret.

While the final days of the Antichrist end in the most terrible war the world will ever experience, the beginning of his reign is quite different. The Bible indicates that the last days will see an initial period of world peace out of which great prosperity will take place. Therefore, we don't see the Antichrist beginning his rule out of the ashes of a world which had just experienced a war with a much greater potential for destruction than all of the world wars combined. Such prosperity would need more than three and a half years of the Antichrist's reign to restore itself to a prosperous and flourishing economy. A reasonable time of peace is required. And we believe the current worldwide peace trend is in line with the signs of the time of Christ's second coming.

"FAMINES, PESTILENCES...."

Famines and pestilences, similar to wars and rumors of wars, don't seem to lend themselves to zeroing in on a specific time. Far from being unique, such things have happened to many generations throughout the ages. Nevertheless, Jesus gave them for us to recognize the specific time of His coming. How then should they be understood?

We believe they are not so much unique indicators as they are qualifiers. Scripture does not say that the signs it gives are "only" for the generation of the end times. But rather, "only" the generation of Christ's return will experience "all" the prophetic signs. So our perspective in considering the last days signs for these times is simply — do we qualify?

Famine and pestilences would seem to be signs (Matthew 24:7) that a technologically advanced age such as ours could eliminate. Nevertheless, even though we are able to produce enough food to feed the world's population, multitudes are still dying of starvation. Famine has been the cause of death for more than 13 million people since 1960.

This century has seen incredible accomplishments in the field of medicine. Modern drugs and vaccines have all but eliminated even the most deadly diseases. For the most part, infant survival and life expectancy rates are on the increase even in the most underdeveloped countries. Yet world health officials are growing in their concern over reports of new diseases and a recurrence of tougher strains of old ones.

One such devastating new disease is AIDS (Acquired Immune Deficiency Syndrome). It has been called "the Black Death in Slow Motion" because of the prolonged length of time it may lie dormant within a victim before his or her immune system is destroyed and death comes. The Black Death killed some 30 million people in the middle ages. The death toll from AIDS is conservatively expected to reach 50 million worldwide in the 1990's if no vaccine or cure is produced. It has been estimated that in the U.S. alone, the deaths of young men already infected will be over one million. That's greater than the American casualty figure for all our wars combined.

"EARTHQUAKES IN VARIOUS PLACES"

The sign that Jesus gave involving earthquakes was not so much that there would be increasingly more devastating earthquakes in the last days, but that they would occur in diverse places. That is what we are seeing today. Not only are many parts of the world experiencing movements of the earth's surface, but they are occurring in places not normally given to such activities. In the United States, the West coast has long been considered to be prone to earthquakes, yet tremors are taking place in the Northeast, the Midwest, and the Southeast. That situation will no doubt lead to greater destruction. For example, the San Francisco area which recently experienced a 7.1 quake suffered the deaths of less than 75 people. Whereas tens of thousands died in unprepared Armenia and northern Iran, both of which had a smaller tremor. Experts fear similar situations taking place in America, especially in major cities such as Boston and New York which have multitudes of buildings and other structures not safe-guarded for earthquakes.

"PERSECUTION AND HATRED OF THE SAINTS"

Not too long ago a high level contingent from the Soviet Union was in the United States to promote Gorbachev's "perestroika and glasnost," the restructuring of Soviet society and a new openness in its attempt to develop a closer relationship with the West. In an interview on a Public Broadcasting System program the leader of the Soviet panel, in answer to a newsman's question over what they felt was the greatest stumbling block to better relations between the U.S.S.R. and the U.S., replied that Evangelical Christianity posed a major problem.[1] His answer, though shocking to some in its candidness, should not be a surprise to those who have long stood against Soviet Communism's militant atheism and persecution of Christians. It is even less surprising to those who take a Biblical perspective of the role of Russia in the End Times.

Yet, the recognition by Soviet officials of the contrary beliefs of Biblical Christianity to their state system is a very limited example when compared to a worldwide anti-biblical system that will eventually come under the control of the Antichrist. As the ways and means of solving the world's problems become increasingly more difficult for Christians to participate in, either because of their religious nature or their ultimate objective, those in charge of such programs will, as the Soviet official did, point to Bible-believing Christians as major hindrances to the global good of all mankind.

While the Bible is not opposed to the "global good," it has very different solutions to bringing about the greatest good for mankind. Its prescriptions are according to godliness and have as their objectives submitting to God's way and glorifying Him. Biblical salvation is found exclusively in Jesus Christ. The world's approach, on the other hand, looks to mankind itself for its greatest good. Man is the final judge of what is good and what is evil. Such an approach glorifies self and seeks solutions in the hope of human potential. As the distinction between the two approaches becomes clearer and the opposition grows, persecution is sure to follow.

Two obvious clashes today involve the issues of abortion and evolution verses creation. We are seeing an ever increasing attempt to improve the quality of life by controlling the population through methods which involve killing unborn children. On a personal basis, abortion is used to terminate a pregnancy for reasons varying from inconvenience to rape. Such methods are being heavily resisted by Christians who are then condemned as being opposed to the rights of the individual and the greater good of society. The battle over the teaching of evolution is also being contested by Biblical Christians primarily because it is contrary to the perspective on the origin of life given in the Scriptures. As a result, some major universities are considering revoking the science degrees of graduates who openly espouse the creation position.

Not as obvious, but potentially more prone to bringing persecution upon Christians, is their resistance to the "authoritative" decrees of psychology. As the "experts" more and more declare the concept of sin and other Biblical teachings to be religious myths and frauds which are detrimental to the well-being of humanity, those who cling to such concepts will be (and already are) viewed as harmful to society. Many have been forced to undergo psychiatric examinations and counseling and some have even had their children taken and placed under the guidance of psychiatric social workers.

Yet it's not that the world will become anti-religious. On the contrary, religion will prosper. That is, as long as individual groups do not promote Biblical teachings which exclude other religions. They must have as a core belief that which will bring them into harmony with all beliefs. So, as Bible-believing Christians resist the coercion towards unity among all religions there is little doubt they will be persecuted as an exclusive sect or cult.

As more and more minority movements increase in their political power and influence, their hostility toward Biblical Christianity will become more prevalent. The Gay Liberation movement, for example, decries the Scriptural believer's view that homosexuality is sin and an abomination before God. The Women's movement declares the Bible to be patriarchal and sexist, and those who believe in it to be anti-women's rights. As these and other organizations with similar antagonisms toward God's Word link up, they will become a formidable instrument in the persecution of Biblical Christianity.

THE LAST DAYS IN THE FAST LANE

In the following chapters we will continue to show evidence of prophetic signs being fulfilled. But, as you shall see, it is not just the signs, rather it's the rate at which they are seducing people which staggers the sensibilities. This generation is being prepared for the last days at almost every level. Current technology, especially in the communication realm, has triggered an information explosion. It has "shrunk the earth." And it has given impetus to the vision of a manageable world government, a solvable solution to all the world's ills. And in the midst of such a world-wide hope, the Bible tells us, will arise a man who will take control. He will be exactly what the deceitful heart of man wants. Scripture calls him the man of perdition, the Antichrist.

12

Preparation For The Substitute Messiah

When Jesus spoke to the disciples as they sat on the Mount of Olives, His statements were warnings to alert those who would be living at the time of His coming not to be led astray by what would take place. His first words were: "Take heed that no one deceives you. For many will come in My name, saying 'I am the Christ,' and will deceive many"'(Matthew 24:4,5). He later said, "Then if anyone says to you, 'Look, here is the Christ!' or 'There!' do not believe it. For false christs and false prophets will arise and show great signs and wonders, so as to deceive, if possible, even the elect. See, I have told you beforehand"' (Matthew 24:23-25).

In earlier chapters we gave examples of the rampant fulfillment of the Lord's prophecies in these times. Yet the multitude of false christs and christ ideas that abound today are only preparatory, a sort of conditioning of the masses to accept the one who will be the ultimate false Christ. He will be, in effect, an idea whose time has come. The Bible refers to him as the Antichrist and it gives very specific details about him.

The book of Revelation tells us that he is a man empowered by Satan (13:2) whose authority will be over the entire world (13:7). He will be like the Caesars of ancient Rome in that complete political, economic, military and religious power will reside with him (13:7,15,17). Also, just as Caesar was worshiped as a god, the Scriptures state of the Antichrist, "all who dwell on the earth will worship him" (13:8) "... or die" (13:15).

The prophet Daniel said that this world ruler will be mighty in power, he will use cunning and deceit to destroy the mighty while he grows in prosperity, and he will magnify himself in his heart. He will destroy the people of God and rise against the Prince of princes, Jesus Christ Himself (Daniel 8:23-26). His self-exaltation will reach a climax as he magnifies himself above all gods (Daniel 11:37). Paul writes to the Thessalonians that this coming "son of perdition ... opposes and exalts himself above all that is called God or that is worshiped, so that he sits as God in the temple of God, showing himself that he is God" (2 Thessalonians 2:4).

THE BRIDE WHISKED AWAY

It is the belief of the authors that those truly committed to Jesus Christ will not be on earth when the Antichrist is revealed. They will be "caught up" or raptured to be with our Lord and taken to heaven as — His bride. Second Thessalonians, chapter two, indicates to us that the Holy Spirit indwelling in believing Christians is the restraining influence on the "lawless one" and it will only be after the bride of Christ is removed that the "man of sin" comes to power. While some argue that the Church will go through the great tribulation and be raptured as Jesus returns to earth at His Second Coming, we don't find that view to be supported by the Scriptures.

Our basic reasons include: 1) The great tribulation is primarily a time of God's vengeance and wrath upon the wicked, not an ordeal to which Christ's bride will be subjected (1 Thessalonians 1:10, 5:9). 2) Nearly all who become believers in Christ during the tribulation are martyred — which would leave very few, if any, to rapture (Revelation 6:9-11, 13:7,15). 3) Jesus describes his returning for the church in terms related to a Jewish wedding ceremony (John 14:2,3). He told His disciples (the bride of Christ) that He was going to His Father's house to prepare a place for them and that He would return for them. He will then take His bride to the wedding feast which is in heaven. The Word of God tells us that takes place prior to His Second Coming to earth to set up His Kingdom (Revelation 19:7,19).

THE FOUNDATIONAL "ONES"

In order for the Antichrist to fulfill all that the Bible says about him, the basic institutions and their programs over which he will rule have to become a practical reality. These are: a one world government, a one world economy, and a one world religion. And it should be obvious to anyone who even occasionally follows the news that political, economic, and religious trends are moving toward globalism, unity, and a new world order that will attempt to better serve the planet earth.

Once the "secret stuff of global conspiracies," today the goal of one world government is openly promoted by leaders from around the world, from former U.S. presidents and cabinet officials, to European statesmen and multi-national corporation heads, to leaders of the United Nations, and, most incredibly, to the present leader of the U.S.S.R., Mikhail Gorbachev. As reported in *Time* magazine in July, 1990, Gorbachev perceives that "all mankind is entering a new age," and in a recent speech mentioned in the same article he recognized the need for "a new world order." That observation, coming from the man whose country many fear as the major stumbling block to any hope of world peace or unity, is staggering in its implications.

Global consciousness and planning have long been the basic objectives of the most aggressive cause-oriented interest groups today, such as the peace movement, the environmental and ecological movements, world hunger activism, and the New Age movement. In almost every area of concern over the complex problems the world is facing, the solutions are being predicated, in most cases, on setting up agencies that have the capability and control to deal with such problems on a global basis.

Books and articles abound declaring the great need for developing a worldwide economic system. The reason is that our present system, or rather, scattered systems, are bringing the world dangerously close to economic destruction. Inflation levels are soaring in some countries, others are in great prosperity, while still others are on the verge of economic collapse. The world's stock markets have fluctuated erratically over the past few years. The debts of many countries are so large they cannot even pay the interest. These critical situations have made the aim of setting up an international monetary system an urgent necessity.

Such a goal is made even more imperative as greater numbers of businesses are scurrying to become part of the expanding international marketplace. The changes in Eastern Europe have brought on a feeding frenzy of involvement from Western businesses. Multi-national corporations are lobbying diligently to bring some form of standardization of trade practices and laws. The great diversity of money systems throughout the globe has long been a source of aggravation for worldwide business concerns, even in these computer assisted days. The time is overripe for development of an economic system which could be brought under the control of a world leader.

As implausible as a one world government and a one world economy may have seemed only a few years ago, the idea of a one world religion still seems impossible. Yet that is the most enthusiastic work of our present religious leaders. The fastest growing religion in the world today, the New Age movement, has the unity of all religions as one of its main objectives. The most newsworthy religious events of the past few years have involved the coming together of diverse beliefs, Christian, Jewish, Moslem, Hindu, Buddhist, Native Indian, and other shamanic and pagan forms of worship, in world prayer days and ecumenical conferences. The primary religious objective for the 1990's, according to organizations such as the National Council of Churches, is promoting the unifying core that lies beneath the superficial differences of many religions: the brotherhood of all mankind and its inherent divinity.

Again, such activities are not taking place in dark corners or secret meetings run by conspiracy groups; they are happening in full view of the world with its blessings. One has only to open his or her eyes to recognize what is taking place — just as the Bible has prophetically stated these things would occur.

DISCRIMINATING IN OUR DISCERNMENT

The apostle John wrote that it is "the last hour, and as you have heard that the Antichrist is coming, even now many antichrists have come, by which we know that it is the last hour" (1 John 2:18).

While the church of Christ will not be around when the Antichrist takes over, it will be, and is now being, subject to the same deceptions and delusions that are preparing the world to receive the "man of sin."

Our concern, therefore, is not so much that the basic structure for the "Beast" is being laid. That is inevitable. But rather that those things, which are part of the indoctrination in preparing the way for the Antichrist, do not ensnare the heart of the committed believer in Jesus Christ and destroy his or her fruitfulness for the Lord. Our theology is quite simple in this regard: True Christians have been saved by grace through faith and created in Jesus Christ for good works (Ephesians 2:8-10). The primary agenda for Satan in the life of the believer is to render him or her ineffectual for God. And that is exactly what happens as a Christian becomes enticed into teachings, beliefs, practices, programs, movements, and so forth, which are not true to the Word of God.

We believe Christians should be very aware that the overall apparatus that will support the Antichrist is rapidly moving into place. But, more importantly, they need to be able to discern the less obvious but more personally damaging devices which are preparing the world for the false messiah. These can have an immediate and destructive impact on their lives. The distinction between such things is a very practical concern. An example of what we mean has to do with those who become preoccupied in their concern about the "mark of the beast." Many have been caught up in a fear over being tricked into taking the mark which Scripture tells us everyone must receive in order to purchase or sell anything when the Antichrist is in power (Revelation 13:16,17).

Although such an event will take place, we don't believe any true Christian living today will be around to be forced to make that choice. And those who come to Christ after the rapture will not be tricked into it. It will be clear cut: Worship the Beast by taking the mark ... or die. So worrying about one's credit cards, social security numbers, the codes on grocery packages, etc., is misdirected attention and misplaced concern. These may, in some way, be part of the technology or system that will be in place during the tribulation, but they have no related spiritual impact on the believer in Christ today.

On the other hand, many Christians have a genuine concern over the environmental problems plaguing the earth. And they should have. "The earth is the Lord's, and all its fullness ..." (Psalm 24:1). All Christians have an obligation to be good stewards of what God has given to mankind (Genesis 1:26-30; 9:1-3). Yet, some Christians in their commendable zeal to do their part may become active in groups in which the leadership promotes the earth as the Mother of us all, with a capital "M". They usually include Nature with a capital "N" and the Sacredness of all life, with a capital "S" signifying the divinity of all life.

For all the earthly good that may be accomplished among such groups, the accompanying religious perspective is in league with the one world religion of the Antichrist and, therefore, spiritually destructive to all who become involved with such a perspective. There is nothing spiritually wrong with doing what we can to eliminate chlorofluorocarbons that destroy the ozone. But it's when such an activity draws one into a belief that is contrary to God's truth that we become part of a false gospel. In doing so we "forfeit God's grace" (Jonah 2:8 NIV) becoming part of the greater problem and not what we were called to be: co-workers with Him in His solution for mankind.

To those who may be thinking "What's the point in doing anything to help a planet in which God is going to devastate by His wrath?", the primary point is — we are to be obedient to God. He hasn't included us as co-workers in His plan of righteous judgment for this earth. There are no teachings in the Bible that condone the abuse of our natural resources. It is man's disobedience, his destructive "better way," that has created the problems. "There is a way that seems right to a man, but its end is the way of death" (Proverbs 16:25). Being obedient first and foremost to what God says we are to do is the only solution.

THE "ANTE" ANTICHRIST INDOCTRINATION

Satan has been preparing the way for "his man" since the Garden of Eden. The very lies that he used to seduce Eve form the foundation upon which the Antichrist will make his ultimate claims. They are found in the book of Genesis and include the denial of the Word of God (3:1), and the potential for immortality (3:4), godhood (3:5), and all knowledge (3:5). In one form or another, down through history, these lies have played an integral part in the formation of mankind's greatest social, philosophical, educational and religious endeavors. And it is, and has been from the beginning, Satan's plan to make his lies the unifying mindset of all who are on this earth.

So by starting with Satan's deception of mankind at the beginning, and considering what Scripture tells us about the "man of lawlessness" to come, we can get a fairly good grasp of what to look for in terms of personal Antichrist indoctrination.

MR. SIX SIX SIX

The Bible uses the numerical symbol 666 for the Antichrist, and volumes have been written speculating about what it means and who it might stand for. Our perspective may be too conservative to add anything new to what has been written, but we believe it is at least implied in the symbol. The number six is representative of humanity. Mankind was created on the sixth day. The book of Revelation states that 666, the number of the beast, is the number of a man (13:18). In Genesis, at man's beginning, Satan offers to mankind the ultimate potential, the realization of its divinity. In the last days before Jesus Christ returns, the Bible tells us that the "man of sin" will be worshiped by the whole world as the ultimate god-man (Revelation 13:8). A major reason why people the world over will freely choose to worship the Antichrist is because he will be recognized as the complete human fulfillment of everyone's divine potential.

THE FRUIT OF DECEPTION

It would follow then, even if the above is only partially correct and these are the days just prior to the Antichrist's coming, that we ought to be seeing the teaching of infinite or divine human potential in all areas of society. And that is indeed the case. To cite just a few major examples we can look to education, business, psychology and religion.

In this century in the U.S., we have all been influenced by the teachings of John Dewey, who has been called the father of American education. He was anti-Christian to the core, a complete humanist, and a signer of the Humanist Manifesto. Humanism's basic view is that "Man is the measure of all things" i.e., there is no god higher than man. The religion of humanism preaches that mankind has within itself all the potential required to solve any and all problems. It has no need to look beyond itself.

In business today, as anyone can attest to who has attended a sales seminar or management conference, the emphasis is upon a positive mental attitude based on the untapped infinite potential claimed to be resident within every human. That belief has been the thrust of increasing numbers of major corporations since the mid-eighties as they have sought the counsel of mind power organizations (Silva Mind Control, Est, now called The Forum, Life Spring, Mind Dynamics, Pacific Institute, etc.) and success/ motivation speakers and programs. The goal is greater productivity through the new realization of man's divine potential (as opposed to the traditional Judeo-Christian view of mankind's inherent sinful nature).

PSYCHOLOGICAL SALVATION

Psychology, particularly psychotherapy, has been the most potent promoter and greatest influence for the teachings that lead to the deification of man. From Freud's psychoanalysis, to B.F. Skinner's behavioral psychology, to the humanistic approaches of Carl Rogers and Abraham Maslow, to today's popular transpersonal psychologies, the bottom line is: man is inherently good. It is external influences that have led him astray: his wrong thinking — his traditional religious beliefs — his father, mother, family — his neighborhood — his culture. Once he realizes his innate perfection he will change his thinking and solve his problems, or so we are told. The goal of psychotherapy is, as one approach puts it, self-actualization— to realize the total wholeness (wisdom, goodness, peace, etc.) that resides within us all and to continually manifest it in our lives. If that is the case then we have no need of a Savior. And, therefore, the belief in a sin nature is the most damning of ideas because it denies the possibilty of psychological salvation, i.e., that all we have to do is look within to save ourselves.

There is a growing number of people who are recognizing psychology for what it truly is: a religious wolf in pseudo-scientific clothing. (For an excellent Biblical evaluation of psychological counseling see: *PsychoHeresy: The Psychological Seduction of Christianity* by Martin and Deidre Bobgan, EastGate Publishers, Santa Barbara, CA, 1987.) That it has strong ties to religion is evidenced by the latest stream of psychology termed "transpersonal." Its emphasis is on the spiritual side of man and life. Yet its religious affinity is not toward the spirituality of Judeo-Christianity, but Eastern mysticism. Men such as University of California professor Jacob Needleman and *Psychology Today's* editor Daniel Goleman have written extensively of Eastern mysticism's close relationship to modern psychotherapy.[1] Goleman quotes an expert in Buddhism and psychiatry who years ago made the informed decree that Eastern religion would come to the West primarily through psychology. The man knew what he was talking about.[2]

13

The Broad Path To The Lie

In the religions of the world today we find perhaps the greatest example of the preparation of the world to submit to and worship the Antichrist. To some that may seem incredible, given the number of very different religions around, but on closer inspection they may not all be so incompatible. As a matter of fact, there is a core belief that is common to practically all non-Biblical religions. It's the teaching that God is in everything and everything is God.

As with Hinduism, which worships millions of individual gods yet sees them as mere diverse representations of Brahman - the Absolute or All (God), so it is with other Eastern religions (Buddhism, Taoism, Shintoism, etc.). God, in their views, is an impersonal force or energy or spiritual power that is in everything that exists and manifests itself in varying degrees in people and other life and non-life forms. So while they may pray to and worship external forms of God in humans, animals, spirits, images and idols, they also look within themselves to find divinity.

Interestingly, scholars have described other major Eastern religions such as Confucianism, Jainism, Theravada and Zen Buddhism as forms of atheistic humanism. They are atheistic because they dismiss or reject the belief in any form of God that would assist in their personal salvation. They are humanistic in their belief that they have all they need for their own salvation within them. Salvation in the Eastern world view is to completely become one with the All.

The relationship to Western humanism should be obvious. If man is the measure of all things then man has all he needs to work out his own salvation, whether that is seen as evolving to a higher stage of evolution (a god-like stage compared to his present state), or reaching a state beyond this finite human world (Nirvana, in Buddhism).

HE'S ONLY MORE GOD THAN THE REST OF US

But how does this relate to conditioning the world for the Antichrist? First of all, when the Scriptures describe him as declaring himself to be God it is not implying that he is claiming to be the omnipotent, omniscient God revealed in the Bible, who created the universe out of nothing and is not part of creation. No created being — angel, demon or man — could pull that deception off. However, what has happened down through the ages is that Satan has successfully instilled in nearly all the religions of the world a perspective of God that the Antichrist (and everyone else, for that matter) can live up to. Eastern religions use this analogy: A drop of water may seem different from the great sea but it's made of the same substance. And when it enters the sea it becomes the sea. So if God is everything, and in everything, then everything is of the essence of God. Therefore man is God; he just has to realize it and begin to live up to the potential of God. The supreme goal of Hinduism is called self-realization — man "entering" into God, realizing that he is God.

In a similar respect, the Antichrist will claim to be God just as everyone is a part of God. But he will demonstrate that he has achieved godhood beyond the wildest imaginations of any human on this planet. This will be aided, the Bible tells us (2 Thessalonians 2:9), through the working of Satan with all power and signs, and lying wonders. And when they bow down to him they will, in effect, be doing what is already consistent with their basic religious belief, i.e., honoring their own infinite human potential.

CONDITIONING THE WEST

The ploy to undermine the truth concerning God's character and divine attributes, as we mentioned in the beginning of this book, has been Satan's most effective strategy. The delusion it has wrought upon man is almost absolute. Second Corinthians states that "the god of this world [Satan] has blinded [their] minds" (4:4). Even in those parts of the world where the major religions (Christianity, Judaism, and Islam) claim to adhere to the Biblical perspective of God, the mass conversions from such beliefs to the god of the New Age is astounding.

The Sufis sect of Islam looks to mystical techniques, its members whirling themselves into altered states of consciousness in order to achieve "union with God." Reformed Judaism like its counterpart, liberal Christianity, have so distanced themselves from the authority of God's Word that many of their leadership claim to be in basic unity with the central beliefs of Eastern mystical religions. The fact that the head of the Catholic church would promote an international day of prayer and invite priests, rabbis, mullahs, ministers, buddhist monks, yogis, gurus, shamans, and witchdoctors to pray for world peace certainly seems to indicate that the pope believes they are all praying to the same God.[1] Or, at the very least, he doesn't recognize their worship as an abomination to the God who has revealed Himself in the Scriptures and stated: "Do not go after other gods to serve them and worship them" (Jeremiah 25:6).

GODHOOD

When the Bible says that we can become sons of God it means that we who are (or were) separated from God by sin, can through faith in Christ be reconciled to God, being "adopted" (Ephesians 1:5) into His family. We become partakers of Christ's divine nature (2 Peter 1:4) only in the sense of taking on His moral virtues, His moral godliness, not His supernatural nature. The teaching that we shall be perfect as God is perfect (Matthew 5:48) has to do with moral conduct and is achieved in Christ (Colossians 1:28; Ephesians 5:27). A perfect man is not a god. And a perfected man does not become a god; he becomes a moral, godly man. If perfection means having supernatural god-like powers and abilities then Adam and Eve would have qualified. They were perfect before they sinned. There would have been no reason, therefore, to accept Satan's enticement to become gods (Genesis 3:5). But they were not gods and the possibility was attractive enough to cause them to disobey God.

Jesus Christ is the personal, infinite God who became a finite man without ceasing to be God. Scripture calls Him the "only begotten of the Father" (John 1:14), "coming in the likeness of men" (Philippians 2:7). While that is a mystery that we can't comprehend, it is reasonable that an infinite God could limit Himself by taking on the form of man. However, it is neither logical nor does the Bible give any support of the idea that finite man can become God, or a god. Rather, it identifies that lie of Satan as the sum and substance of rebellion. "I am the Lord your God ... you shall have no other gods before Me" (Exodus 20:2,3).

NEVERTHELESS: "CHRISTIAN" DIVINITY

All the cults of the West conform to the basic teachings that are preparing us for the False Messiah. Though many claim to be Christian and claim the Bible as their primary text, they hold to none of the principal doctrines of God's Word in practice. Mormonism is a primary example.

Mormons, like Hindus, believe in many Gods. They also believe that by being faithful to Mormon teachings, they are working their way to becoming Gods. In Mormonism, there are three Gods over this world: God the father, God the son, and God the holy spirit. God the father was appointed by the heads of the Gods to rule over this particular world. There are supposed to be millions of worlds just like this one and every faithful Mormon male shall also become a God the father over one of those worlds. According to Mormon teaching, God the father is an exalted physical man. For those millions who are true to the Church of Jesus Christ of Latter-day Saints then, the feasibility of accepting a physical man such as the Antichrist, who claims to be God while recognizing that potential in everyone, will be entirely consistent with the main objective of their theology.

Christian Science and other Mind Science cults (Unity School of Christianity, Religious Science, Science of Mind, Divine Science, etc.) are Western variations of Eastern mystical religions. To them, God is not a personal Being but rather an all-pervasive Mind, a "divine spark" of which resides in us all. The Universal Mind is not worshiped as a person but is approached as the Law of Mind which can be "scientifically" manipulated. Those in the Mind Sciences, therefore, do not pray as one would to a personal God. They affirm or declare positively those things they want, first by thinking it in their own minds. That is supposed to affect the Universal Mind (God), causing it to bring about the reality of their affirmations. As we have indicated above, believers in the Mind Science religions share a great deal in common with Buddhist humanists. They are self-deified, atheistic humanists, working out their own salvation by their positive thinking and affirmations.

Ideas and teachings of the Eastern and Mind Science religions are rampant almost everywhere one looks today. They are prevalent in medicine, chiropractic, psychology, education, business and religion. They are promoted as reality manipulating techniques that will solve the world's ills. From curing cancer to losing weight, to achieving sales goals, to improving one's golf game, to easing stress, to increasing faith, to you name it ... and claim (affirm) it. Such ideas are the basis for Positive Mental Attitude (PMA), Visualization, Self-image Psychology, Success/Motivation techniques, Norman Vincent Peale's Positive Thinking, Robert Schuller's Possibility Thinking, and Positive Confession.

DECEIVING THE ELECT, IF POSSIBLE

The major appeal of the Mind Science cults, although they claim that spiritual reality is the only true reality, has centered in their emphasis on material prosperity and physical healing. "Prosperity is your divine right" affirms the bumper sticker motto of one Religious Science organization. Mary Baker Eddy, the founder of Christian Science, "borrowed" many of her teachings from the man who helped heal her back pains, a metaphysical healer named Phineas Parkhurst Quimby. Both Charles and Myrtle Fillmore, the founders of Unity, claimed to have been healed of tubercular diseases through Mind Science principles. And Ernest Holmes, who began Science of Mind, taught that mankind lacks happiness, health and wealth because it is largely "ignorant of the Law of God which governs all things." Their teachings are incredibly seductive and they have made great inroads into Evangelical Christianity. (For complete documentation of this charge, see Dave Hunt and T.A. McMahon, *The Seduction of Christianity*, Harvest House, 1985.)

The founders of Unity and Religious Science were very open about the fact that their teachings were taken from the cream of all the world's religions. Both Ernest Holmes and Mary Baker Eddy boasted that their own religious perspectives would be, in Holmes' words, "The great new religious impulsion of modern times [especially] ... in its capacity to envelop the world."[2] They were right. Though not because of their particular genius or their cult, but because they simply furthered the gospel of the Antichrist. And it is particularly alarming to see Mind Science teachings "envelop" those who claim to be Bible-believing Christians.

The fastest growing movements within Evangelical Christianity are those which have been heavily influenced by Religious Science doctrines. Under the various labels of Positive Confession, Word of Faith, Faith Message, Rhema, etc., these movements manifest strikingly similar methods and philosophies to the Mind Sciences. A major part of their emphasis is on healing and prosperity. Like Holmes' Law of God, they teach the Law of Faith which governs all things and must be understood and applied correctly in order to "conceive and believe and receive" what you want. They believe, as does Unity, that the ultimate laws governing the physical universe are spiritual and are available to those (Christians and occultists) who learn and apply them.

The Evangelical "faith" teachings are very similar to the Mind Science ideas regarding sickness — it should not occur in the Christian's life. They claim that Christ's crucifixion (His atoning work on the cross) ended all sickness and disease for Christians. Therefore, the only reason a Christian can possibly become sick is because he or she is lacking in the faith required to maintain good health. Should one become sick, however, healing is brought about based on the amount of faith one applies to the situation. Some teach that even acknowledging that one is sick will cause the illness to continue or worsen. The mental thought is supposedly a form of faith. If one thinks "positively," healing takes place. "Negative" thinking, such as recognizing and admitting that a cold is getting worse, for example, brings about whatever the thought concerns. Therefore, they claim that a Christian is never to describe the symptoms of an affliction even in prayer. He is to positively affirm or claim the healing. These are views highly consistent with the approach of all healing practitioners in Christian Science.

"FAITH" gODS

Another major heresy finding support among the Positive Confession/Faith teachers is the belief that Christians, having been born of God, become gods under God their Father. According to their teachings, Adam and Eve were the original gods of this earth. However, they lost their godhood and their dominion over the earth when they sinned. Satan then became the god of this world and it is the function of every Christian, whom it is claimed is a potentially reborn god, to take dominion back from God's adversary, the Devil.

The restoration of dominion to Christians can only be carried out by those who realize their potential as gods in God's class. The very laws and techniques that God uses to create, such as speaking things into existence, are likewise to be used by those in "God's class" who are mastering the law of faith through the technique of positive confession. Some of the teachers support their belief in godhood on the basis of spiritual birth arguing that just as dogs have puppies and cats have kittens, so God must have little gods. Other such teachers contend that because God is spirit and men and angels are also spirit beings, then being sons of God must include being part of God.

Such a development within Evangelical Christianity is a sure sign that we are in the apostasy of the last days. The blatant disregard for or twisting of the clear teachings of Scripture, by teachers who claim to be Bible teachers, is just as staggering as the blasphemy involved. Considering the above, as we have pointed out in another context, if Adam and Eve were already gods, Satan's offer to them of godhood would have been a waste of time.

Regarding being a part of God, if mankind, angels, and God are all connected because they have the same spiritual essence or makeup, then whatever is spiritually true about men and angels is also true about God. If I am part of God and I'm a sinner, part of God must also be a sinner. If an angel is part of God and rebels, becoming a demon, then part of God is a demon. God then cannot save us or solve our corruption because part of Himself is also corrupted.

The clear revelation of the Bible is that God is totally separate from His creation. God is Spirit (John 4:24). But His Spiritual essence is uniquely eternal and divine. The makeup of humanity and angels includes a spirit element, but it is created spirit — neither infinite, eternal (our spirit had a beginning) nor divine. It is also corrupted by sin (2 Corinthians 7:1). God, therefore, not being a part of sinful humanity, can and did bring salvation into the world through His sinless and perfect Son, the only true Messiah, Jesus Christ.

Nevertheless, the conditioning of the world is growing in order to prepare hearts and minds for the false messiah, the Antichrist. And to that end God's adversary, Satan, has not left any areas to chance. That self-deified man to come, the demonized minister of the Devil, will appear as a minister of righteousness (2 Corinthians 11:14,15) and reflect the greatest desires of the ones being prepared to bow down to him. In him they will initially see their own personal potential. In the pages ahead we will explore many of the ways and means those desires are being induced and facilitated.

14

New Species For A New Age

The Psalmist asks of God, "What is man that You are mindful of him?" (8:4). God's answers throughout the Scriptures, contrary to some popular views, are not the fertile ground from which self-esteem can blossom. In summary, we find that man is a sinner (Romans 5:12), a rebel whose very nature is hostile toward God (Romans 8:7), whose own righteousness is as filthy rags before Him (Isaiah 64:6). He is under condemnation. The penalty is death (Romans 6:23). He is destined to eternal separation from God and everlasting torment (2 Thessalonians 1:9).

Yet while man was still God's enemy, God Himself, not because of anything found in man but because of God's own character, made a way for man to be reconciled to Him (Romans 5:6, 8-11). God became a man, in the form of Jesus Christ, and took upon Himself the penalty due every human (1 Timothy 2:5,6). Those who freely choose God's way of salvation, accepting by faith the sacrifice of Christ's death for their sins, become new creations in Christ. Those who have done so have been restored to God and the purpose for which they were intended: To share in His love, function according to His good pleasure and will, and to glorify Him (Ephesians 2:1-10). To accomplish His purpose in humans, God indwells and empowers the believer in Him by the Holy Spirit to live life as it was intended (Romans 8:9-11).

Also, they will live eternally with Him (John 3:16). He will never leave them nor forsake them (Romans 8:35-39). Such is salvation for the new man, woman, and child in Christ.

THANKS, BUT NO THANKS

According to the Scriptures and confirmed by common observation, most of the world is not interested in God's free gift of eternal life, which cannot be earned by man's works but comes by grace through faith in Jesus Christ (Ephesians 2:8,9). Despite the Biblical pronouncements of futility, mankind is bent on a course of working out its own salvation. All religions not true to the Bible, whether those seeking the help of a deity (or deities) or those which are atheistic, shunning deities in favor of their own self-efforts, have salvation as their chief goal. The same applies for seemingly nonreligious philosophies of life, morals, and ethics, as well as theories of origins, means of existence and death. Scientism, for example, is the belief held by some (mostly scientists) that all the answers to life will be discovered within science. It's a religious belief. Although the religious and so-called nonreligious views, ways and means seem to be very different, most end up with basically the same ideas.

The theory of evolution has both a religious and nonreligious background. It is perhaps the foremost example of the world's "thanks, but no thanks to the Creator for His way of salvation." For it has been seized by man to explain God away. On the other hand, it has been used historically to explain God. It can be found in some form in the oldest non-Biblical religions, from Hinduism to the earlier but lesser known mystical, occultic and animistic (spirit worshiping) systems. The ancient religious idea is that somehow the deities spawned primitive entities which over the aeons of time evolved in complexity from lower to higher life forms. Aided by the gods through millions of lifes and rebirths, through plant, animal and human stages, the material life of the universe was believed to have evolved upward to the realm of the gods, the realm of spirit or pure consciousness.

GETTING IT DOWN TO A SCIENCE

Though Charles Darwin is regarded as the father of the (so-called) science of biological evolution, the central ideas go back as far as the Greeks, four hundred years before the time of Christ. They believed that some form of sea matter produced life. The resulting life forms then evolved in complexity to support themselves on land. Darwinian evolution is, for the most part, only a more detailed theory: Life came from non-life. It started by accident. It continued gradually over billions of years. Primitive forms, through the mechanism of chance, evolved into more complicated forms, from which evolved even more complex forms. Evolution theory basically decrees that all life is connected through its process — minerals (inorganic substances) evolved to single cells which became plants which evolved to animals which evolved to humans. Humanity is thus far regarded as the highest stage of evolutionary development by most evolutionists. But there are some who are convinced there is a higher stage.

SOME BASIC PROBLEMS

However, before we get into higher evolutionary theory it would be good to consider some of its basic problems. Darwin's theory has been promoted for almost a century and a half and has become "the law and a fact of science" in education today. While many educators say, "that's as it should be," it seems that "they haven't done their homework."

First of all, many evolutionists promote the idea that all life has resulted from an explosion. It has been called the "Big Bang" theory and it states that the universe began in an unfathomable blast which took place in an instant in time. That chance violent burst set forth all the elements and processes necessary to randomly bring about the universe as we know it today. Or so it is claimed by faith. But the observable evidence proves that chance explosions do not produce order. Therefore, considering the magnitude of the universe, it takes far less faith to believe it's possible to produce the Encyclopedia Britannica from an explosion in a type manufacturing plant.

Secondly, testing a theory scientifically involves observation. But no one was around to observe life's beginnings. There are no examples of life being randomly produced from non-life which have been observed taking place today.

The third problem has to do with missing links, those forms that show clearly the evolution of say, a cat to a dog, one distinct kind of animal to another. Cogs and dats are still missing. After more than 125 years of aggressive searching, no examples of transitional creatures showing the direct connection between different species have ever been found.

Fourthly, there are a number of life maintaining organs and processes in the makeup of living things that could never have evolved. They have to have all the necessary parts in place in order to function. Considering the circulatory system, for example, how was life sustained while the heart was "waiting" on all its own parts and other parts to evolve to the stage necessary in order to pump blood?

The last basic problem to be included here (for there are many others) has to do with chance. According to mathematics, which is the backbone of science, it is not possible for life to be randomly generated (by chance) from non-life. In other words, it can't happen by accident. The ordered complexity of the makeup of even the simplest cell (mathematically and reasonably) demands the involvement of an intelligent designer. Complex structures that make up a cellular unit must all exist in perfect order or the cell cannot exist. There is no rational way to conceive that nonliving material can assemble itself to become complex ordered mechanisms. Adding great lengths of time does nothing to help the situation. Without the ingredient of some form of intelligence to bring about order, the generation of life forms is a mathematical impossibility.

WHAT ABOUT BIBLICAL EVOLUTION?

There are some people around who think that evolution is the process through which God brought about creation. It is an interesting perspective, but true neither to the Bible nor evolution. The god of Evolution is time plus chance. No intelligent help required. The God who reveals Himself in the Bible, however, points to the design of creation as irrefutable evidence that He, the Omnipotent Creator and Designer, exists (Romans 1:20). The book of Genesis makes a big point that God created life "according to its kind." It's found nine times in five verses (1:11,12,21,24,25) and that is the way we find life now and in the fossil record. For those trying to make a case for "Biblical evolution," there is no mention of "catdogs or cogs" in the Bible. Nor does it give even a hint of reference to Adam and Eve's ape-like parents.

Evolution theory's major contribution to modern society has been to effectively blind people to their only source of truth. Its impact on Christianity has been to sway believers away from the reliability of God's Word so greatly needed in their lives. Many have turned to what the Bible calls "oppositions of science falsely so-called" (1 Timothy 6:21) to help supplement what our Creator's Word clearly and absolutely teaches. And its impact on the great commission (Matthew 28:19) has been to help slam the Bible shut before a missionary can get started. How so? Try witnessing to someone who tells you he or she can't believe a book which is so blatantly misinformed right in its opening sentence: "In the beginning God created the heavens and the earth."

ONWARD AND UPWARD

Biological evolution theory is pseudo-scientific, meaning it sounds like science, it looks like science, it acts like science, it even has bits and pieces of science in it. But it's not science. It is actually religion posing as science. It is a form of scientism, which consists of beliefs formulated by men of science that have no true basis in science. None of evolution's major truth claims are, or can be, derived by the scientific method. Its speculations on the origin of life and its transitions, which supposedly took place over billions of years, and which no evidence indicates is continuing today, can only be accepted by faith. Similar to some of the Eastern religions which are atheistic/humanistic, such as Theravada and Zen Buddhism, evolution also has its doctrines concerning the destiny of man.

It is claimed that if the process of evolution stopped it would eventually result in the extinction of all life. For the species to survive it must continue its upward advancement. Man's evolution, for example, is supposed to have demonstrated a natural progression from primitive beast to scientist. At least that's the popular idea, though the Bible indicates otherwise. It claims that at the time of man's creation he was perfect; even after sin altered his nature, he was superior in many ways to man today. How many people today have been around for eight or nine hundred years? Noah was 600 years old when the flood took place and he lived 350 years afterward. Mankind has just recently attained to a life average in the high 70's. Nevertheless, we are told that evolution is moving the universe onward and upward.

Species have progressed to higher levels. If man is the highest evolved species, a naturally progressive question would be: Where to next?

Darwin believed the fact that man had evolved to his present state and held great hope for the species to reach an even higher destiny. Others have pointed out that since man has risen from an amoeba (a single cell organism) there's no limit to what he will become. Dr. Robert Jastrow, former director of the highly revered Goddard Institute for Space Studies, suggests that evolution on other planets could be billions of years ahead of us. Therefore life forms elsewhere could be far beyond the flesh and blood stages of humanity. He speculates that they could be pure minds, akin to what we refer to as spirits, having incredible intelligence and powers by our standards. They might seem as gods to us.[1]

SEEDS OF HERESY

The co-father of modern evolutionary theory with Charles Darwin was Alfred Wallace. You don't hear too much about him because he was an embarrassment to the promoters of hard core material (only matter exists) evolution. Wallace was into spiritualism — the belief that disembodied intelligences exist and can be contacted. He recognized that biological evolution alone could not account for the nonphysical aspect of man: his consciousness, which is the totality of his thoughts, feelings, and impressions. He argued that since man's consciousness was not physical, it is reasonable to conclude that it could continue on after his physical death.

Though still clinging to Darwinian evolution as the gospel, many disciples today are sounding like grandfather Wallace. Some hold that mind, thoughts, emotions, etc., are things generated by the physical brain, and can only be products of such a material mechanism...on the one hand. On the other hand, many are thinking and saying that somehow it may be possible for such things to exist independent of the physical body. Perhaps thought is the real substance of the universe. The new physics is professing such ideas. And suppose consciousness itself has evolved? Whatever the case, these are heretical times for the faithful followers of biological evolution.

HAVING HIS CAKES AND EATING THEM

Satan plays all sides when it comes to promoting the delusion of his ultimate lie — that man is, or can become, a god, or God. As the Scriptures point out, the lie was born in his heart (Isaiah 14:14) and sold to Adam and Eve (Genesis 3:5). Satan subsequently has infused it into all false religions and atheistic/humanistic teachings which will contribute to the acceptance of his definitive example of man as God: the Antichrist (2 Thessalonians 2:4). Amazingly, it doesn't seem to matter how contradictory the ideas are. Godhood, New Species, Higher Intelligences.... They all somehow come together to help feed the delusion.

Material/biological evolution is a prime example. It teaches that a "man is god" and claims there is no higher species on earth. Though at odds with one of the professed mechanisms by which evolution works — chance — evolutionists see man as having the potential of directing his own destiny, which is certainly a trait of a god. Nevertheless, modern evolution theory, strictly speaking, is opposed to any idea of nonphysical reality. Yet that hasn't seemed to bother many of the mystically oriented religions and religious movements which point to it as "scientific proof" for their spiritual doctrines. Leading New Age theorists are heavy-handed in convincing people that the "fact" of biological evolution proves the "fact" that man is evolving toward higher consciousness. New Ager and evolutionist Dr. Jean Houston holds workshops and seminars for leading world and U.S. policy makers. Her program has them relive in their imagination man's evolutionary beginnings, through the primordial past, up to the present, then guides them towards evolution's potential future phase — which involves higher consciousness.[2]

THE NEXT STAGE: THE EVOLUTION OF CONSCIOUSNESS

What exactly is higher consciousness? Well, no one knows exactly. But there are enough individuals, groups and organizations around today pushing it as the great hope for mankind that one can put together a good idea of what they have in mind.

Let's start with normal consciousness. It is the common awareness state in which people normally operate. It includes our usual mental activities, thought processes, feelings, and emotions. It is a function of the interaction of mind and body (many, including us, add spirit).

Higher consciousness, as its believers claim, is a purer way. It bypasses the need for the mind to interact with the brain and nervous system in the thought process. It is supposed to be beyond the thinking process altogether. Supposedly, it's a state of instant knowing. An illustration would be to consider someone taking flying lessons, with all of its required study, practice, and physical apparatus, just to get a foot off the ground. Contrast that with someone else who simply steps into the sky and soars wherever he wants. The first is normal consciousness compared to the second, higher consciousness. Sounds great.

A major reason, we're told, that higher consciousness is being advanced today is because mankind isn't doing so well in his normal state of consciousness. We're not to feel guilty though, the condition of man is not so much a fault of his own. Instead, it seems his problem is that he is on the threshold of an evolutionary transformation of consciousness. It's been compared to the physical trials, tribulation, and transition of labor a woman experiences just before she is about to give birth. However, this new stage of evolution, it is affirmed, will make such tribulations all worth it. But you have to wonder....

The "science" of biological evolution, as we've said, has been an incredibly damaging deception. Billions of research dollars have been spent on pursuing the myth. It has added to the overwhelming devastation, pain and sorrow of mankind. Though claiming that humanity is the highest of the species, the theory has actually reduced man to the level of an animal. And if the theory is true then why should there be an outcry against men and women acting like brute beasts? Why don't evolutionists themselves defend such activities. After all, an animal acts by natural instincts, not morals.

If evolution is indeed true then why wouldn't even the most militant evolutionist simply excuse the gang who robbed his house, raped his wife and killed his children as acting naturally? Couldn't it have been merely an instinctual demonstration of the survival of the fittest? Perhaps such a gang had not yet evolved high enough. Or perhaps the next evolutionary phase will be better. Maybe higher consciousness is just what mankind needs. And then again, maybe not... especially since it's being sold to us by the same agent who booked us for the evolution trip.

15

The Higher Consciousness Trip

Reaching states of higher consciousness is one of the main objectives of the New Age, but it's not a new deal. Neither is the New Age for that matter. Higher consciousness has long been the chief goal of Eastern religions. It is also called by other terms, including God consciousness, cosmic consciousness, cosmic-at-oneness, enlightenment, and self-realization. It usually involves entering an altered state of consciousness, that is, going into a trance-like state.

There are many techniques for experiencing higher consciousness, from the ancient to the modern: meditation, yoga postures, chanting, special breathing practices, rituals, concentrating on crystals, drugs, hypnosis, and biofeedback. However, the technique induced experiences are temporary because only at death (permanent separation from the body) is higher consciousness reached absolutely and eternally. Termed "moksha" in Eastern mysticism, it is believed to be the state of total salvation where finite beings merge with the Infinite. So it is claimed that techniques can only give physical man mere tastes of this "heaven" while they help both to condition him and to aid him in his work toward it.

All the forms of yoga have been devised to give its practitioners glimpses of higher consciousness and to get them to the permanent state. Contrary to what the YMCA catalog says, hatha yoga is not for health, it's for death. The yogi practices certain physical techniques which are designed to help prepare his spirit being for what he hopes will be the final separation from the bondage of his physical body. The word hope is used because if he's not ready at death, he must reincarnate over and over and over again until he is ready. The law of karma demands that all wrong acts committed in past lives must be worked off in this life or future lives until the slate is clean. Yoga is the Hindu system for working off what is needed to satisfy the law.

A Christian or anyone else who practices yoga — even just for the exercise — is on the work path to "yoking" himself or herself to Brahman, the highest Hindu concept of God. Yoga means union with the Absolute Reality (the impersonal God-force). So, at the very least, it is a blatant form of idolatry. In addition, its breathing, postures, and meditative techniques are contrived to help empty the mind in order for one to experience God-consciousness.

HAZARDS ALONG THE PATH

The way to higher consciousness usually involves a method of removing all conscious thoughts from the mind, vacating it of everything that would hinder one from experiencing his or her oneness with the All. And while the various techniques are said to give one a foretaste of Ultimate Reality, the different methods also open one up to other experiences. Healings are claimed. Incredible abilities and powers are demonstrated. Deities are contacted. Spirit guides are enlisted. Demons afflict (physically). Insanity occurs. Suicides take place. To anyone who cares to read through the literature by the ancient teachers of the various meditative paths to higher consciousness, he or she will find many such experiences — and warnings. It's a hazardous road to Nirvana.

What the New Age movement is in the process of doing is repackaging and reselling all the old occult techniques. Consumer label warnings are not to be found, but not to worry, at least modern chemistry, high tech devices and medical professionals have been enlisted. Synthetic drugs do all and more than the American Indian shaman's (medicine man) sacred mushroom and cactus drugs. Biofeedback devices are called electronic yoga machines because people have experienced the same altered states and contacted similar entities through them. Hypnosis has been instrumental in enabling people to check out their past lives so they can take care of negative karma in this one.

Harvard medical teams are studying Tibetan meditation and promoting variations as relaxation techniques for stress. Visualization, the ancient mystical technique for creating reality and contacting spirit guides through mental imagery, is being sold by medical experts as a method for curing cancer. (For an extensive critique of these and other New Age practices and techniques, see T.A. McMahon and Dave Hunt, *America: The Sorcerer's New Apprentice*, Harvest House, 1988.) The way to higher consciousness and godhood, by New Age reckoning at least, seems to be more positive than negative. So, aside from a bad trip or two along the way, what could be the problem?

THE HIGH CON JOB: PREPARING MINDS

An altered state of consciousness is a risky situation. First of all, it's not normal — or natural. It is imposed upon the mind. The yogis, Tibetan monks, Sufi dervishes, and Zen Buddhists all work at it, training themselves to facilitate entering an altered state. But as one guru said, "There are the long paths (hard work, discipline) and the short paths (drugs, electronics, hypnosis, total submission of the will) to godhood." The short paths are West's most popular ways of inducing an altered state. Many who took hallucinogenic drugs during the hippie decades, for example, had experiences of higher consciousness. Such "short" trips convinced thousands, who had no knowledge of the teachings of Eastern religions, that they had experienced God. Many have since turned to meditation and other methods to pursue higher consciousness.

By design, an altered state of consciousness is supposed to render the mind available (and vulnerable) to outside influence. The religious intent is to open oneself up to God, or the deities. But there is plenty of testimony, both ancient and modern, that "less trustworthy gods or spirits" sometimes get involved. An example of how such a thing might happen is found in hypnosis. Though it's not a science, and no one really knows how it works, it has been used enough to get a handle on the process.

The person to be hypnotized submits his will to the hypnotist, allowing himself to be led into a trance or altered state of consciousness. The person's mind then becomes open to the will of the hypnotist who gives him suggestions, instructions, commands, etc. Some say that the will of the person being hypnotized cannot be violated, but research experiments have proven otherwise. In order to be hypnotized, one's will must be effectively submitted at the beginning of the process. The hypnotist's instructions are then carried out, not on the strength of the person's own will, but on the strength of the hypnotist's imposed command, i.e., his will. People mostly turn to hypnosis because they lack the "will power" to either stop or control certain habits such as smoking, drinking or overeating. So their new success at mind control then certainly seems to be from the power of suggestion induced by an outside mind.

It seems reasonable to conclude that the key to the hypnotic process is an altered state of consciousness which opens a person to outside influence and control. The will of the person is given up in such a state. The mind becomes a blank screen, likened to a computer which can be programmed with instructions, or even to a television screen, which can receive visual programming. But the critical question is, "Who or what does the programming?" You may say it is the hypnotist. But what of those mystics who meditate their way into an altered state of consciousness and receive information from deities? And what of the visions and images experienced in such a state?

THE ULTIMATE MIND TRAP

Eastern meditation seeks to empty the mind of all normal conscious thought in order to experience God, and to finally merge with It. The Absolute, we're told, cannot be known through the physical senses. You have to "experience" It. But the fact that the meditator must use his normal consciousness to be aware that he's had the experience makes one wonder how much "higher" the consciousness actually is.

On the other hand, the meditation described in the Scriptures involves active thinking and reasoning — not "emptying" one's mind. The psalmist writes, "I will meditate on Your precepts and contemplate Your ways" (119:15). The God of the Bible declares, "Come now, let us reason together" (Isaiah 1:18). God wants us to use the natural faculties He gave us to consider Him. His primary communication with us is through His Word which requires thinking in order to understand what He wants us to know. To that end, He has revealed a great deal about Himself to us in the Bible which He exhorts us to read and continually think about.

No one merges or literally becomes one with the God of creation. He is separate from all that is made. Nevertheless, the Bible tells us that God, through His Holy Spirit, resides within all who come to Him by faith in Jesus Christ (Romans 8:9). While God's residency within us is a mystery, it is not mystical. We don't become God. Neither does God become us. Yet God's residency in the believer enables him or her to go beyond just knowing about Him. It is the basis for developing an intimate relationship with Him, and to experience His love and other attributes in a personal way (John 14:16,17).

OTHER MINDS

So our perspective is that the promise of the path to higher consciousness is not just greatly suspect, it is the ultimate mind trap. And our concern has many good reasons. To go back to our example of hypnosis, if the hypnotist is supposedly able to implant a suggestion in a counselee or client's mind, why couldn't a secretary who just stepped into the room? Or the window washer? Or a demon? Who says not? After all, one's will has been yielded to the spirit/mind of the hypnotist. Isn't he transferring thoughts to another person's open thought processor? Who says someone or "some thing" else couldn't intervene?

And by the way, who made up the rule (as we have been told) that only medical, or psychological, or better yet, Christian medical/psychological personnel can administer hypnosis in a safe, ethical, non-occultic manner? Hypnotism is, was, and always has been occultic. And spirits, more precisely demons, don't play by man's rules. Altered states of consciousness are the most effective mental states for programming, even controlling the minds of humans. And the evidence is massive that Satan and his demons are the ones who are the actual "audio" and "video" programmers.

THE WILL PLAYS A PART

We are of the opinion that the will is crucial but not an absolute guarantee of protection against an unsaved person being controlled by Satan. If that were not so, what would prevent demons from possessing all humanity, including those before they come to salvation? Some might suppose that Satan wants as many as possible to worship him freely. In Deuteronomy we do find that false worship involved the worship of demons (32:16,17), and the book of Revelation points out that the people would not repent of their "worship[ping] demons" (Revelation 9:20). Yet it seems to be consistent with the Scriptures that God restrains him and his demons (Job 1:9,10) except when someone voluntarily turns his will over to demons through various idolatries and occult techniques and devices.

People who use drugs are not always demonized, though drugs have historically been used to contact spirit entities. Those who are anesthetized by drugs for operations, or those who get drunk once in awhile don't necessarily become possessed, as far as we know. Normally, in such cases, there is no intention to turn the will over to a spirit as in the obvious (and even disguised) religious meditative forms, ritual drug use, and hypnosis involving altered states of consciousness. While their wills may play a part in shielding them from demonic takeover, we also know that the abuse of drugs leads to addiction — which is the near total collapse of the will. So at the very least, drugs can have a conditioning effect on the will of humans.

There are other types of situations that do not involve an altered state of consciousness yet can lead humans into demonic possession. The use of the Ouija board, as one example, doesn't involve an altered state of consciousness. Often the activity includes a person in a normal state of consciousness initially desiring communication with a nonphysical entity. Then, in the process of seeking more information after the initial contact, the person often times submits his will to the entity. Contact with spirit entities is condemned in the Bible because they are all demons who are intent upon leading humanity to destruction (Deuteronomy 18:10-12). That is the reason Paul wrote: " . . . I do not want you to have fellowship with demons" (1 Corinthians 10:20). Such fellowship allows demons the opportunity of breaking down a man's will, which is part of their basic program (2 Timothy 2:26; 2 Corinthians 11:3).

IT'S HIS PROGRAM

Both the road to and the final destination of higher consciousness has Satan's tracks all over them. In addition to the yielding of the will through the altered states process, the programs fed to the highly receptive mind, which openly promote his basic lies, are a sure indication that he produced them. In the case of the mystic, for example, his will is surrendered as he opens himself to merging with a deceptive concept of God. The tribal shaman, ingesting ceremonial hallucinogenic drugs, gives himself over to spirit guides in the form of power animals. The New Age channeler allows himself to be a trance vessel controlled by entities which claim to be "higher intelligences." Meditative groups tune themselves into disembodied extra-terrestrial intelligences who say they have evolved beyond the human species and will guide the planet into its next phase. These are only a handful of the thousands of related programs being dispensed through the bait of higher consciousness today.

THEY'RE HIS PRODUCTIONS AND PRODUCTS

For all that's been written about the social impact of material evolution, its most devious work in this century has been to set up the times for the biggest, most widespread spiritual/mystical revival in human history. This was accomplished primarily in two ways. First, evolutionary science has failed miserably to live up to its claims of solving all mankind's problems. Clearly science is, and has been, a disappointing savior. Also, to add insult to injury, it has created just as many or more problems than it solved. It has caused many to look elsewhere. Secondly, it has been amazingly successful in restricting things spiritual from Western civilization's diet. Over a span of some one hundred years a great hunger has developed. Today the appetite for the spiritual/mystical is ravenous. Enter the New Age, served up on the empty platter of evolutionary theory.

Though it has no shortage of aliases (The Holistic Health, Traditional Healing, Human Potential, Higher Consciousness, New Consciousness, Shamanism, Perennial movement, etc.), the New Age movement could also be called "Satan's Supermarket." Through it Satan has brought together and put on display every scheme, technique, teaching, and product that he has ever devised for seducing mankind since the Garden of Eden.

Satan has refurbished so many things related to his basic lies that even the old taboos are big sellers today. There seems to be something for everyone's fancy: meditations, gurus, rituals, totems and take home idols. Witchcraft and magic — white, black or natural. Satanism — worshipful or humanistic. Occultism, sorcery, wizardry, divination, spiritism, chantings, fortunetelling, acupuncture, mediums, tarot cards, psychics, mandalas, astrologers and astrology kits, Ouija boards and every size crystal. Those who turn to such things have made a commitment to rebellion. As the prophet Samuel declared, "For rebellion is as the sin of witchcraft, and stubbornness is as iniquity and idolatry. Because you have rejected the word of the Lord..." (1 Samuel 15:23).

But what of those who are "not into all that mystic/witchcraft junk." If the path of higher consciousness doesn't suit, what about the path of Self-improvement? Step right this way....

16

The Self Trip

Mankind has always been interested in itself. We look out for self. We feed self. We wash and clothe self. We love self. Both historical and contemporary awareness bears witness to the fact that an individual's own needs and comforts are a natural priority of humanity. That's why the commandment was given: "You shall love your neighbor as yourself" (Matthew 22:39). It is a variation of the golden rule: Treat others as you want to be treated. You love and care for yourself, not wanting to be mistreated, so treat others the same way. The Word of God recognizes such self-interest or self-love in the heart of every human (Ephesians 5:29). While it identifies self as a universal characteristic, it never extols it as something to be developed. On the contrary, the Bible treats it as sort of a blighted section of a garden: it's possible though difficult to root out, but by all means keep it from spreading.

However, to His disciples Jesus said, "If anyone desires to come after Me, let him deny himself, and take up his cross, and follow Me" (Matthew 16:24). To some that simply means giving up certain things that are not good for them. Others have even likened it to monastery life — cutting oneself off from worldly temptations. But actually, it is far more radical. Jesus' command to his disciples to deny themselves has to do with them ceasing to live their lives in their own strength, in their own wisdom, in their own way, and according to their own will. Jesus was to be their example: "Father... not My will but Yours, be done" (Luke

22:42). "I can of Myself do nothing. ... I do not seek My own will but the will of the Father who sent Me" (John 5:30). They were not to look to self, but to Him for "all things that pertain to life and godliness (2 Peter 1:3). They were to take love beyond the golden rule.

Jesus instructed them, "A new commandment I give to you, that you love one another, as I have loved you, that you also love one another" (John 13:34). He promised His love would flow through them; His love, not something born of our fleshly nature. John, the apostle, writes: "In this is love, not that we loved God, but that He loved us and sent His Son to be the propitiation for our sins" (1 John 4:10). And again, "By this we know love, because He [Jesus] laid down His life for us. And we also ought to lay down our lives for the brethren" (1 John 3:16). The heart of Christianity is sacrificial love. The practice of Christianity is the same: "Husbands, love your wives, just as Christ also loved the church and gave Himself for it..." (Ephesians 5:25).

The emphasis of Christianity is not toward self, but toward others. "Let no one seek his own, but each one the other's well being" (1 Corinthians 10:24). "Be kindly affectionate to one another with brotherly love, in honor giving preference to one another" (Romans 12:10). "We then who are strong ought to bear with the weaknesses of others, and not to please ourselves. Let each of us please his neighbor for his good, leading to edification. For even Christ did not please Himself..."(Romans 15:1-3). Again, Jesus is our ultimate example: "Christ Jesus... being in the form of God... made Himself of no reputation, taking the form of a servant... humbled Himself... to the point of death, even the death of the cross" (Philippians 2:5-8).

We are told in 2 Corinthians 5:15 that Jesus "died for all, that those who live should no longer live for themselves, but for Him who died for them and rose again." We are to turn from self to God, loving Him with all our heart, soul, and mind. That is our first duty. The second is to love our neighbor (Matthew 22:36-40). Both are directed outward, not inward to self.

KEEPING UP WITH THE WORLD

Christianity today has turned to the gospel of self-preoccupation. Self-love, self-esteem, self-acceptance, self-image, self-confidence are all being promoted as Biblical. We concur. However, we see this in the light of prophecy as the fulfillment of Paul's warning to Timothy concerning the last days. He writes in 2 Timothy 3:1,2: "But know this, that in the last days perilous times will come: For men will be lovers of themselves...." Many have not given much heed to this Scripture as a sign indicating we are in the last days before the return of our Lord. But we think it is one of the proofs-positive.

First of all, you can search hard and long through secular history books, church history and the Bible and not find a generation which comes close to fulfilling that prophecy — by today's standards. Why do we say that? Because until the mid-nineteen hundreds it was considered bad to be selfish and good to be unselfish. Certainly there have been selfish people making up different societies, but when have there been common teachings spanning the globe advancing selfishness as important to the psychological health of mankind?

Some may not like the term "selfishness" but it accurately describes what is taking place. We didn't invent the phrase "the Me generation." Neither did we suggest titles for popular magazines such as *SELF* or *US*. Nor was the advertising slogan "do it for yourself... because you're worth it" our idea. Psychology is the source here, telling us to esteem, love, forgive, unconditionally accept, be a friend to, like, be affectionate toward, and indulge — ourselves. According to its theories, it seems for too long mankind has nurtured a brooding hate for itself, especially in Western society. This was primarily the fault of Judaism and Christianity, which promoted the idea that man was sinful and wicked. We are told that such religious misunderstandings of man's inherently good nature have done great damage to numerous generations.

NOT EXACTLY HEAVENLY INSPIRED

The philosopher Friedrich Nietzsche, who taught a "God is dead" and "man is Superman" philosophy, considered Christianity beneath contempt and Christians spineless. He twisted the Scriptural teaching of "loving your neighbor as yourself" to mean Christians don't truly love others because they don't really love themselves enough. His challenge started the church off in a scramble to correct the "problem" even though it was misrepresented and non-existent.

To those, however, who think Nietzsche was "on to" something because they know some people who hate themselves and can't love others, we would have you answer this question: Is it really themselves they hate... or their circumstances? Except in rare situations, which we will mention later, all people love themselves. A woman who feels that her nose is too big, or that she has a funny body shape, or that no one likes her, may act as though she hates herself. She may become upset and depressed. But the truth of the matter is she hates her circumstances. And the reason she's upset is not because she hates herself. Something hurtful is affecting someone she loves. Do people normally get depressed when bad things happen to people they hate?

Nietzsche's accusation that Christians don't love themselves enough in order to really love others has a host of other problems. Self-love leads not to looking out for others or loving others but to self-preoccupation. All the selfisms do. Common sense tells us that our everyday phrases describe what's going on with people who work at loving themselves. They're said to be "full of," "hooked on," or "enamored with" themselves. There's no built-in U-turn in self-love. It's an extremely narrow and never ending road in the direction of self. Christians only have to think of the opportunities they have willfully bypassed regarding reaching out to others or witnessing of God's love. More often than not it was due to being ill-at-ease, or there was a fear of embarrassment. We call that "being self-conscious." On the other hand, individuals who forget about themselves, who are always doing things for others — we matter-of-factly refer to them as "selfless."

THE GOSPEL ACCORDING TO PSYCHOLOGY

The other major influence from outside the church regarding self-love was atheist psychologist Eric Fromm, who was also a humanist. Amazingly, he, like Nietzsche, influenced liberal and then evangelical seminary professors and pastors to accept his interpretation of the Bible on self. That's akin to having two wolves explain the sheep safety procedures to the shepherds. Fromm wrote about and interpreted the same scripture as Nietzsche, also insisting that self-love was severely deficient in society. This he blamed on Christians misunderstanding the Scriptures. He said that since we are to love another self (neighbor), we are also to love our own self, because the love of self includes all selfs. There was a certain seductive logic to it.

Many Christian leaders bought it, adjusted it a bit, and even arranged it according to the latest and most popular psychological theory. They took Fromm's count — (1) love neighbor and (1) love self — and added the part of that related Biblical text which Nietzsche and Fromm objected to, that is, (1) love God. The three commandments were then (by way of Christian psychology) lined up with humanistic psychology's founding father's (Abraham Maslow) "hierarchy of needs." We now have promoted among Evangelicals this popular "Scriptural" teaching on self-love: We have to first, love ourselves, second, love our neighbor, and then we can, third, love God.

Turning to the text, however, we find that the first problem in interpretation is math. There are only two commandments given. Love God and love your neighbor. In Jesus' words, "On these two commandments hang all the law and the prophets" (Matthew 22:40). The clear intent of the second commandment

— after first, loving God — is to look to the welfare of others as you already do for yourselves. It is a reminder of our natural tendency toward taking care of number one, a characteristic which needs no encouragement. That is the perspective throughout the Bible and there are many admonishments regarding it, including these: "For all seek their own, not the things which are of Christ Jesus" (Philippians 2:21); "Let each of you look out not only for his own interests, but also the interests of others" (Philippians 2:4).

SETTING THE RECORD STRAIGHT

In the apostle Paul's prophetic statement referring to men becoming "lovers of themselves," it could easily have been translated "self-affections" or, as we're used to hearing today, "feeling good about yourself." That's what it means in the Greek. And our experience has been that when this point is brought up some people immediately react to it with aggitation. The cry sometimes goes up: "So what's wrong with feeling good about myself?" And others may add: "Am I supposed to feel bad about myself?" Or regarding what we wrote earlier: "If I'm not supposed to love myself, then they must be telling me to hate myself."

No, we are not. That's neither possible on our own nor is it the Biblical option. Loving God and living for Him, and loving others and putting them before ourselves is the command. As we obey Him He will fill us with His joy and His love to the overflowing, and we'll become less and less preoccupied with ourselves. He will see to our needs. Most of us know the Scripture: "But seek first the kingdom of God and His righteousness, and all these things shall be added to you" (Matthew 6:33). Left to our own devices we miss "Him who is able to do exceedingly abundantly above all that we ask or think..." (Ephesians 3:20).

FEELING GOOD ABOUT MYSELF

And to the question of "What's wrong with feeling good about ourselves?", we want to answer it with a question. Is it possible to feel good — without feeling good about yourself? Suppose someone you didn't know, or didn't know you, picked your name out of the telephone book and gave you a terrific gift, no strings attached. Wouldn't that make you feel good? But would you feel good about yourself? On what basis? Our point is, it is possible to feel good, even incredibly happy, without taking credit for it.

But some might say, "It's fine to feel good, but what's wrong with feeling good about ourselves — about building ourselves up?" To that the Scriptures reply: "Unless the Lord builds the house, they labor in vain who build it" (Psalm 127:1). Self is a false foundation. "For no other foundation can anyone lay than that which is laid, which is Jesus Christ" (1 Corinthians 3:11).

The same goes for a self-image. Our own image is vanity; reflecting His image is what we were created for. And again, who will take credit? "Not that we are sufficient of ourselves to think of anything as being from ourselves, but our sufficiency is from God" (2 Corinthians 3:5); "And what do you have that you did not receive? Now if you did indeed receive it, why do you glory as if you had not received it?"; "He who glories, let him glory in the Lord" (1 Corinthians 4:7; 1:31).

The Scriptures say that each of us is like an earthen vessel. We can shape it, decorate it, and fill it with self... doing our own thing so, hopefully, we can feel good about ourselves. Or — we can do it God's way: "But we have this treasure in earthen vessels, that the excellence of the power may be of God and not of us" (2 Corinthians 4:7). We can be a high priced, worldly acclaimed and greatly coveted piece of porcelain...for a time, maybe. Or, we can be an unself-conscious earthen vessel filled with the glory of God.

Concerning self-hate, which we alluded to above, it is an impossibility for man who has turned from God to self. Self, in fact, is such a person's substitute god. Again, it is a person's reaction to objectionable circumstances that are upsetting to self that psychology has interpreted as self-hate. But the reality is self cannot be truly hated by those who turn from God. Self is the only hope they have left, even though it is a false hope. Therefore, the psychological perspective that self-hate is widespread is both an illusion and a delusion.

There are rare examples of self-hate given in the Bible and they only took place, and can take place, by God's grace. Self-hate only occurs when God (for only He can) pulls back the veil covering man's heart and opens a man's eyes to see the depths of his sin nature in comparison to God's righteousness. Certain individuals in the Bible were given such insights into the extensiveness of self's rebellion against God and its utter depravity (Isaiah 6:5; Romans 7:24). Job, whom God called a righteous man, also got a glimpse of it and said, "Therefore I abhor myself, and repent in dust and ashes" (Job 42:6).

DENYING SELF: A SCARY PROPOSITION

The Biblical self teachings are, especially in this day, very difficult for many of us to receive. It isn't only because of the erroneous self promotions that seem to be everywhere either. They wouldn't be popular if they didn't hold some interest for the heart of mankind. In blunt language, self concepts tell us that we've got what it takes to get what we want. That appeals. It also seems comfortable. You don't have to give up anything. You can have your cake and eat it too. Or at least that's what many today are being led to believe...or want to believe.

Denying self, on the other hand, doesn't have a natural appeal. It means giving up something. Trusting God. For the non-Christian, the Christian in name only, and even those believing

Christians who have one foot on the self path, it's a scary proposition. But it's God's way. For anyone who desires to be a true follower of Jesus, it is the only way. And Jesus speaks to our fears: "Come to Me, all you who labor and are heavy laden, and I will give you rest. Take My yoke upon you and learn from Me, for I am gentle and lowly in heart, and you will find rest for your souls. For My yoke is easy and My burden is light" (Matthew 11:28-30). The reason His yoke is easy is because He enables us to carry it. "... it is God who works in you both to will and to do for His good pleasure" (Philippians 2:13). And His good pleasure is our best possible pleasure.

17

Self-Esteem And Perilous Times

When Paul wrote to Timothy concerning the "perilous times" of the "last days," his first statement was that men will be "lovers of themselves." As we said in the last chapter, by that he meant men would be focusing their affections upon themselves, feeling good about themselves, and esteeming themselves. This self-orientation is far beyond what Jesus was referring to when He spoke of loving your neighbor as you do yourself. It relates to all of today's selfisms: self-esteem, self-image, self-acceptance, self-worth, etc.

It is important to be aware of the grouping into which Paul places "lovers of themselves." Contrary to the teachings of psychology, including so-called Christian psychology, self-esteem is not the solution to all mankind's problems. We believe Paul, inspired by the Holy Spirit, placed "lovers of themselves" first because it was the principal underlying cause of the things he listed afterward. He wrote, "For men will be lovers of themselves, lovers of money, boasters, proud, blasphemers, disobedient to parents, unthankful, unholy, unloving, unforgiving, slanderers, without self-control, brutal, despisers of good, traitors, headstrong, haughty, lovers of pleasure rather than lovers of God, having a form of godliness but denying its power. And from such people turn away!" (2 Timothy 3:2-5).

Paul's list includes the fruit of those who have become "lovers of themselves ... rather then lovers of God." That a major part of the Evangelical church would propose self-esteem as a solution to mankind's problems — in light of the overwhelming Biblical evidence to the contrary — is one more proof to the authors that we are in the days of delusion, deception and apostasy which Jesus predicted would occur prior to His return.

DARKNESS FOR LIGHT

The prophet Isaiah had strong words for those, Christians included, who would turn the truth of God's Word upside down, teaching that which He says is sinful and destructive as though it were good. "Woe to those who call evil good, and good evil; who put darkness for light, and light for darkness; who put bitter for sweet, and sweet for bitter!" (Isaiah 5:20). The self life is indeed bitter. Think of anyone you know that is bitter. Self is the preoccupation which keeps them in bondage.

The lie is that turning to self sets you free... "to be the person you want to be." Incredibly, self teachings are the cornerstone of many therapy programs which deal with problems of addiction. The idea is that people turn to alcohol and drugs because they don't like themselves. Though it seems to us to make more sense that people turn to drugs to feel good (self-indulgence), either "just for kicks" or to temporarily blot out the circumstances that upset self. Nevertheless, building up self-esteem is seen as the key. Once they have a better image of themselves, it is said, there will be no need to turn to drugs. There are a number of drug prevention programs aimed at young people which take such an approach. The catch phrases include: "Get high on yourself, not drugs"; "Just say NO to drugs." Building up self, it is believed, will help enable one to refuse to use drugs.

On the contrary, Paul writes that those who turn to the self life are "without self-control" (2 Timothy 3:3). The solution, according to Paul (who wrote of his own struggles with self), was turning one's life over to Jesus Christ (Romans 7). Only He can enable us to do what we ought. Self-control is the fruitful outcome of turning one's life over to God's Holy Spirit. "For if you live according to the flesh [sinful nature] you will die; but if by the Spirit you put to death the [sinful] deeds of the body, you will live. For as many as are led by the Spirit of God, these are sons of God" (Romans 8:13,14).

SORRY, WRONG IMAGE....

The contemporary cultivation of self is the concluding preparation of the soil from which Satan will reap a harvest. Hearts and minds are being prepared to bow down to the Antichrist — who will be a self-deified man. The beginnings of selfism within mankind were a result of succumbing to the lie of godhood, and that original sin of rebellion wrought immediate problems. Adam and Eve, the first two people to be created in the image of God, and who unself-consciously lived for God, began looking out for their individual self-images after they sinned. Adam blamed Eve; Eve blamed the serpent. Both of them became self-conscious of their nakedness and their sin and hid from God. But God found them and mercifully offered the solution to their problem.

God's plan of redemption presented in the Bible does not include building up man's image of himself so that he can confidently stand in the presence of God. Being made in God's image, we are to be a mirror reflection of His moral qualities, His godliness. It's only His image that has true value. Besides, a mirror is supposed to reflect an image other than itself. Yet we, as mirrors, are being taught to create our own images. The only way that can happen in the case of a real mirror is for it to be bent around so that it can reflect itself. And as anyone who has been in a carnival funhouse can tell you, bent mirrors produce distortions.

FROM SELF TO SALVATION

God's plan is to bring man back into a distortion-free, right relationship with Him. It involves our admitting to Him our sinfulness and inability to save ourselves. We are to accept by faith Christ's death as the payment for the penalty for our sins, a penalty required by an absolutely just and righteous God. When we take that simple step of faith the Scriptures tell us: "... whoever believes in Him will receive forgiveness of sins" (Acts 10:43). Christ's work, and His alone, is the basis for our reconciliation to God. All we have to do is turn to Him in faith. "Let the wicked forsake his way, and the unrighteous man his thoughts; let him return to the Lord, and He will have mercy on him; and to our God, for He will abundantly pardon" (Isaiah 55:7).

Sometimes a person may consider that his or her sins are too great for God to forgive. Such a confession though is actually a reverse form of pride. The person may not be thinking it through, or may be caught up in esteeming even the sinful self too highly. Whatever the case, what is actually taking place is God is being told that the death of His Son, His grace and His mercy are not sufficient for an individual's particular sin.

A variation of this takes place when someone says, "I know God forgives me, but I can't forgive myself." Again, such thinking is the product of today's selfisms and self-preoccupations. Self, in such an instance, has been exalted above God and His Word. The person will not submit to God's Word on forgiveness, about which David writes, "... cleanse me from my sin. ... Wash me, and I shall be whiter than snow. ... Make me to hear joy and gladness..." (Psalm 52:2,7,8). The Bible never addresses forgiving oneself because that is absurd. Self is the sinner here. It sinned against God, and perhaps another person. It has no function in the forgiving, only in the asking for forgiveness. So asking and not being willing to receive forgiveness nullifies the asking.

SELF TO HIGHER SELF

It has been observed that while history has recognized numerous individuals who claimed to be gods (kings, caesars, pharaohs, some religious leaders, etc.), that idea hasn't really trickled down to common man until modern times. One reason for its slow advance could have been the practical problems involved. Being a god, by general understanding, involves having one's own autonomy; that is, self-determination and self-rule. A god does its own thing. The more gods you have, the greater the potential for clashes of wills resulting in ongoing conflicts. Greek and Roman mythology gives vivid illustrations. The gods were always fighting; the top gods were always having trouble with the lesser gods.

So man has devised ways of keeping Satan's lie of godhood alive, while avoiding at least some of its problems. In India, for example, the goal of Hinduism is to realize that the individual self is God. That includes everyone. But what kept the people in subjection was a hereditary religious/social class system, called a caste. The priesthood was at the top, and the system even included a category outside the caste for those who were considered the lowest of the low. The general idea here is that although all individual selves are part of God, some are closer to realizing they are God. The priests, being the most "spiritual," were therefore submitted to by those of the lower castes, and non-castes called untouchables. This kept a lot of potentially unruly gods in line.

SELF HEADS WEST

At the present time, the caste system is being substantially eroded and fewer people are striving to work their way up (through reincarnation) to higher class levels. Gurus and other self-proclaimed holy men are taking over, offering quicker ways for all to realize godhood and reach Nirvana. Interestingly enough, the different paths of the gurus all require submission to themselves. The guru is god, they all say, and their methods will, they all claim, direct one to his or her higher self.

It is nothing less than mind-boggling to consider that millions and millions of people in the West's once traditionally Judeo-Christian society have readily submitted to a handful of Hindu gurus. But then again, the carrot of enticement has worked from the beginning: You shall be as gods. The pitch is to self and for self and is practically guaranteed to attract anyone who is not more interested in, in Jesus' words, "deny[ing] himself," and following after Him, the only true God.

GOD'S WAY VERSES THE LIE

Some people see no difference between an Eastern mystic's self-denial and what Christ taught. Some even fear Christ's words because of the misunderstanding. The difference is the mystic denies his individual self (called atman) so he can merge with God (Brahman, the ultimate Self). In the process, he empties his mind of all things regarding himself and others, waiting for what he believes is an experience of becoming indistinct from, or one with, God. The giving up of self may seem unselfish, but it's totally self-serving. Besides seeking God-consciousness experiences and powers, the mystics are trying to finally achieve a state of nothingness: no desires, no feelings, no thought, no hunger, no pain, no suffering, no awareness — and no one else considered. A Hindu holy man sitting in a yoga position for hours upon hours in meditation is not the Biblical picture of self-denial. The goal of the mystic, yogi, guru, swami, etc. is to ultimately get himself out of the misery of this physical world.

A Christian's perspective of self-denial is as a vessel eternally committed to Christ for His glory and the benefit of others. A Christian allows God to mold and shape himself or herself as God pleases. The desires of one's heart are given over to Christ to conform to His desires. There is never a mindless vacuum involved in which God comes in and takes control. It is a continual daily process of saying "no" to self-will and "yes" to God's will. Though heaven for the Christian is certainly free of the misery of this world, that aspect is not even worth comparing to the gloriousness of being with God, and with others who love Him, for all eternity.

THE GREAT SELF DELUSION

The reason we keep pointing to the religions of the East is because they contain most of the beliefs and teachings which are transforming Western culture. The New Age, the fastest growing religious movement in the world today, is based upon an Eastern mystical perspective. Psychology, which is absolutely dependent upon self being innately good and therefore self needing no other savior, sees an Eastern world view as necessary for mankind to find lasting mental health. Education is totally committed to the Eastern principles of religious humanism. Science, which is breaking out of its materialism mode, is turning to mysticism for answers. Medicine, as well, is on an Eastern holistic path of healing the body, mind and spirit.

In order to understand the times we all have to be aware that our society is knee-deep in a post-Christian/early Eastern mystical era. We have to recognize that major aspects of our culture are reflecting ideas and concepts which are militantly opposed to Biblical Christianity. Such ideas may shun their religious clothing, often disguising themselves in secular forms. But they have one singular purpose: To prepare the hearts and minds of men, women and children to receive the Antichrist, the one who will demonstrate that he has realized, far beyond anyone's dreams, the goal of becoming a god. People the world over will certainly be in awe of him, but their hearts will tremble at an even more awesome prospect. To borrow a godhood phrase from Mormonism, "As man now is, God once was; as God now is, man may become." Self can indeed become a god... or so it will seem to "all who dwell on the earth" (Revelation 13:8).

18

The Maranatha Preparation

These days before the return of Jesus are both the best of times and the worst of times. And it will continue to be that way for both believers in Jesus Christ and those who reject Him.

For those of us who are followers of our Lord, Jesus Christ, living in the time of His coming ought to be tremendously exciting. Jesus Himself encourages us in that excitement. "Now when these things begin to happen, look up and lift up your heads, because your redemption draws near" (Luke 21:28). And it is a time for the special equipping of God's people: "... on My menservants and on My maidservants I will pour out My Spirit in those days" (Joel 2:29). Seeing things unfold according to the prophecies of Scripture and knowing that soon and very soon we will be with Him, should make our hearts race with great expectation.

At the same time, there will be increasing problems for those who have a heart for the righteousness of God. Just as Lot was distressed by the wickedness in Sodom, so too will the committed Christian be distressed as he is subjected to the rising depravity and anti-Christian sentiments and activites of a world being conditioned for the "man of rebellion." Persecutions will come for those who cling to Jesus Christ, His Word, and His way (John 15:20). Nevertheless, by the grace of God those who are steadfast in the faith will abound in good works and fruitfulness, "count[ing] it all joy when [they] fall into various trials..." (James 1:2).

PEACE, PROSPERITY AND GODHOOD

There will be genuine excitement as well for those who are drawn to the spirit of the Antichrist. They will initially rejoice in the seemingly great progress the world is making toward solving all its problems. The accompanying rise in wickedness will be rationalized by psychologists and sociologists as merely the throwing off of the last chains of an oppressive, sin-minded Biblical era. These grossly deceived "experts" will agree that such anti-social behavior will pass when people understand the underlying cause of such actions. People will be persuaded that their negative thinking, stemming from thoughts of things like sin, guilt and judgment, has led to the denial of their innate goodness. But those in charge will confidently maintain that even the worst offenders will all be changed. The latest refinement of the many mental control methods, consciousness altering techniques and mind therapies that are becoming acceptable even today, will most assuredly correct wrong thinking.

Optimism will run high because individuals will be convinced that their life's directions have only very positive options. Gone will be the threat of accountability to a personal God, a coming judgment and eternal hell fire and brimstone. Such "negativism" has even now given way to the wonderful possibilities of a higher self, a higher evolution, a higher consciousness, and men and women realizing their divinity, becoming the gods and goddesses they were meant to be.

THE "COSMIC GOSPEL"

The "infinite human potential" message will come from every information source on the face of the earth. Plus elsewhere... especially from elsewhere. Contact with other worldly minds through trance state techniques (meditation, drugs, hypnosis, sensory deprivation, etc.) is already commonplace and spreading rapidly. Whether they call themselves deceased loved ones, spirit guides, ascended masters, more highly evolved entities, or extraterrestrials, their message is the same.

Researchers of such communications received while people are in meditative states of consciousness have found a remarkable consistency in the information. They've dubbed it the "cosmic gospel."[1] No matter who contacts the nonphysical entities, no matter what the culture, or how far removed from society-at-large, the supposedly different entities always get around to basically the same teachings. These include: "We are guiding mankind in its upward evolution."; "Man is now at the threshold of higher consciousness."; "All is one, we are all connected."; "Humanity is divinity."; "Self is a part of God."; "All you need is within you."; "Death is an illusion."; etc., etc. This basic storyline is remarkably similar to the one the serpent fed to Eve in the Garden of Eden. The source then was demonic and the content of the messages bears witness that the source hasn't changed.

THE NEGATIVE SIDE OF THE STORY

When the world accepts the rule and religious worship of the Antichrist, it will accomplish many of its own desires. The initial progress will be similar to that of the unified and humanistic people who desired to build the city and Tower of Babel, contrary to God's will for them. "And they said, 'Come, let US build ourselves a city, and a tower whose top is in the heavens; let US make a name for OURSELVES...'" (Genesis 11:4). The Scriptures tell us God looked down on them and acknowledged that success would follow their working together as one. But He would not allow them to complete the task which was born in rebellion and would ultimately result in mankind's destruction.

We believe that the attempt by the Antichrist to unify and build up the world has the same humanistic goals that were strived for in building the Tower of Babel. Man, committed to doing his own thing, will attempt to demonstrate his self-proclaimed godlike potential. But this time the God of all creation will allow the "man of iniquity" (empowered by Satan) and all those who bow down to him, to take their best shot at transforming the earth into paradise. Mankind can do some amazing things, as this century has demonstrated. But as we have also seen, the planet is paying dearly for most of them. And that will be the way the scenario unfolds, in our opinion, for the first three and a half years after the Antichrist comes to power. Early successes will eventually warp and crack under the strain of the very devices that seemed to bring them about.

Turning to self, as we pointed out in the last chapter, brings about selfishness and a host of other self-generated evils. As the Scriptures indicate, such a time will see society and families corrupted by those who are "brutal, despisers of good, traitors, headstrong, haughty, lovers of pleasure rather then lovers of God" (2 Timothy 3:2-5). "Now brother will betray brother to death, and a father his child; and children will rise up against parents and cause them to be put to death" (Mark 13:12). No one will be able to think, confess, affirm, or visualize this rising tide of wickedness away.

Turning to sorcery, magic (black and white), witchcraft, divination, astrology, and other forms of occultism, will bring millions of people into direct contact with demons. Isaiah warns this new Babylonian generation, which has practiced magic and sorcery since their youth, that their occultism will not save them from the destruction and judgment that will come upon them (Isaiah 47). The same fate will befall those who get caught up in the revival of traditional healers such as medicine men and shamans, and spirit religions such as Voodoo and Santeria.

For all of the drug preventative promotions and programs that abound today, the Scriptures indicate that drug taking (called sorceries) will be rampant prior to Christ's second coming (Revelation 9:21; 18:23; 21:8; 22:15). In ancient times sorcerers took drugs to contact spirit entities in order to obtain favors and power. Then and now the activity has led, and will lead, to terrifying bondage. Drugs have long been a major doorway to demonic possession.

THE DEMON FACTOR

Some people are under the false impression that hell is a place where people go and are tormented by the devil and his demons. The truth is "the lake of fire" is the place where demons will suffer their own torture. It was created for them after they rebelled against God. And those humans who join Satan in his rebellion are condemned to the same place and fate. "Depart from Me, you cursed, into the everlasting fire prepared for the devil and his angels [demons]" (Matthew 25:41).

Demons won't be torturing anyone in hell — but they will on earth. "Woe to the inhabitants of the earth and the sea! For the devil has come down to you, having great wrath, because he knows that he has a short time" (Revelation 12:12). We believe that at a point half way through the seven year tribulation the most devastating and destructive acts mankind has ever been subjected to will take place. Satan and his demons, knowing they have failed in trying to rival God, and knowing where they are headed, unleash the fury of their total depravity upon all humanity. They will go down wrecking and destroying, taking whomever they can with them. But that will only be a small portion of what, at that time, "the inhabitants of the earth" will suffer.

"PARADISE" LOST, AND THEN SOME

"Unless the Lord builds the house, they labor in vain who build it" (Psalm 127:1). As the initial successes and excitement of the Antichrist's work begins to fade, that Scriptural fact will take its toll on those who partake in the Antichrist's humanistic attempt at creating paradise on earth. But the evidence that it is not working will be the least of man's concern. The Bible calls the time of the Antichrist's rebellious works the "time of the Lord's vengeance" (Jeremiah 51:6) or the "great tribulation." This refers especially to the period after the Antichrist "sits as God in the temple of God, showing himself that he is God" (2 Thessalonians 2:4). That act is called the "abomination of desolation" (Matthew 24:15) and Scripture describes what immediately follows: "For then there will be great tribulation, such as has not been since the beginning of the world until this time, no, nor ever shall be. And unless those days were shortened, no flesh would be saved" (Matthew 24:21, 22).

THE POURING OUT OF GOD'S WRATH

It is hard to imagine a time more devastating to mankind on the earth than the worldwide flood of Noah's time. Only eight humans survived. But even a casual reading (if that's possible) of just chapters six, eight, nine and sixteen of the book of Revelation will make the difference between His former and latter judgment very obvious. By comparison, those who perished in the flood suffered only a relatively quick physical punishment. In the "great day of His wrath" (Revelation 6:17), however, the suffering and torment will be of greater length, intensity and diversity.

At one point during the great tribulation the superficial peace that came without making peace with God will take a hard fall. A fourth of the earth will die by the sword, by hunger, by disease and the beasts of the earth (Revelation 6:8). At another point a third of the trees are burned up, all the grass, and a third of the creatures in the sea die. A third of the rivers and springs are poisoned, and the sun, moon and stars are drastically altered (Revelation 8).

Then a third of all mankind die; all sea life perishes; the sun scorches men with great heat (Revelation 9 and 16). Those who take the mark of the beast and worship his image are afflicted with foul and loathsome sores (Revelation 16:11). For some, even death will not be an option for escape. "In those days men will seek death and will not find it; they will desire to die, and death will flee from them" (Revelation 9:6).

GOD: PATIENT, BUT ALSO RIGHTEOUS AND JUST

There will be untold millions who will turn to God for salvation during the seven years of the tribulation period. There will be the ones who did not previously believe in Jesus Christ before He raptured His followers and took them to heaven. John writes of these tribulation saints, "they did not love their lives to the death" (Revelation 12:11). And their blood will flow.

Their martyrdom is part of the reason for God's wrath. Those who bow down to the Antichrist will destroy and murder the saints of Christ with a vengeance; and God will avenge them. "For they have shed the blood of saints and prophets, and You have given them blood to drink. For it is their just due" (Revelation 16:6).

God tells us in His Word that He does not want anyone to perish (2 Peter 3:9), and desires that everyone would be saved (1 Timothy 2:4). Even when He afflicts, it is for the good of salvation (Psalm 66:11, 12). Yet while many receive eternal life during the tribulation, an even greater number of people harden their hearts to the free gift of salvation made possible by Christ's death on Calvary's hill. They want it their way or no way, adding even greater wickedness to their overflowing depravity. "But the rest of mankind, who were not killed by these plagues, did not repent of the works of their hands, that they should not worship demons...and they did not repent of their murders or their sorceries [drugs] or their sexual immorality or their thefts"; "And they blasphemed the God of heaven because of their pains and their sores, and did not repent of their deeds" (Revelation 9:20,21; 16:11). God is indeed longsuffering with His creation.

THE MARANATHA FACTOR

Maranatha means "Our Lord comes!" When the apostle Paul used the phrase he added it after a statement regarding man's opposition to the Lord Jesus Christ. "If anyone does not love the Lord Jesus Christ, let him be accursed. O Lord come!" (1 Corinthians 16:22). And that is what happens at the end of the tribulation period. Jesus, in His second coming, returns to deal with the opposition. He comes back not as the sacrificial Lamb which He was in His first coming, but the conquering King. "Behold, the Lord comes... to execute judgment on all, to convict all who are ungodly among them of all their ungodly deeds which they have committed in an ungodly way, and of all the harsh things which ungodly sinners have spoken against Him" (Jude 14,15).

Christ's enemies are drawn to a place called Armageddon (Revelation 16:16) and it is there He will deal finally with all the opposing armies of the world. "Then the Lord will go forth and fight against those nations, as He fights in the day of battle" (Zechariah 14:3). "And I saw the beast [Antichrist], the kings of the earth, and their armies, gathered together to make war against Him [Jesus]..." (Revelation 19:19). All who stand in rebellion will be slain. All but two, that is.

The Antichrist is captured alive, along with the false prophet, the one who performed many of the deceptive miracles and caused people the world over to take the mark of the beast (Revelation 13:11-17). The Bible says, "These two [will be] cast alive into the lake of fire burning with brimstone" (Revelation 19:20). Satan will not suffer that same fate until a later time. However, He will be bound and restrained from the earth until the end of the one thousand year period of Christ's physical reign.

ARE YOU EXCITED?

Maranatha! The Lord is coming! And He is coming first for His bride, the church. If that thought doesn't send even the briefest sensation of joy through your nervous system, heart and mind, you had better check your heart. Have you trusted in Christ? Are you living for Him? Do you see in your own heart the love of Christ as compelling as that which will be in the hearts of the tribulation saints — those who did not love their lives, even facing death for His sake? Do you love life more than Jesus?

As we have stated elsewhere, there are more verses in the New Testament referring to the return of the Lord Jesus Christ than on any other one subject. God therefore must surely want us to give it a lot of consideration. If we do so, God will graciously begin to fill our hearts with whatever we may have found lacking in our honest answers to the questions raised above.

To reiterate an important point made in earlier chapters, we believe that all those who are "saved by faith" (Romans 10:9,10,11,13) will be caught up to be with the Lord in the clouds when He returns for his bride, the church (1 Thessalonians 4:17). They will not be on earth when the Antichrist comes to power. They will be in heaven with Christ through the days of "the fierceness and wrath of Almighty God" (Revelation 19:15). They will also be with the King of kings and Lord of lords at His glorious second coming. "See, the Lord is coming with thousands upon thousands of His holy ones..." (Jude 14 NIV). "These [of the Antichrist] will make war with the Lamb, and the Lamb will overcome them, for He is Lord of lords and King of kings; and those who are with Him are called, chosen, and faithful" (Revelation 17:14).

19

The Maranatha Preparation - The Best Part

All the different parables and direct teachings that deal with the coming of the Lord offer similar exhortations and instructions: Get ready! Be prepared! Keep watch! Don't be deceived! Wait upon Him! Holdfast His Word! Be blameless! Purify yourself! Keep doing according to His will! Keep doing good works! Live soberly, righteously, and godly! Establish your hearts! Love His appearing! Eagerly look for it! Pray for His return!

Considering just the above sampling then, it is incredible that there are major movements (called Kingdom/Dominion, Restoration, Reconstruction, Latter-rain, Manifest Sons of God, and so forth) within the church which ridicule Jesus' coming to rapture His bride off this planet. One of their common arguments is that the idea of a rapture breeds an escapist mentality. Supposedly those who believe in it will become "do-nothings," sitting around waiting for their quick exit out of this fallen world.

To the contrary, the doctrine of the rapture encourages believers to action in the Lord, so they will be found well pleasing to Him when He appears. In the book of Titus we find, "... denying ungodliness and worldly lusts, we should live soberly, righteously, and godly in the present age, looking for the blessed hope and glorious appearing of our Great God and Savior Jesus Christ" (2:12). Anyone who becomes a do-nothing — whether claiming to believe in the rapture or not — is sinning. "But be doers of the word..."; "... to him who knows to do good and does not do it, it is sin" (James 1:22; 4:17).

Since the rapture can take place at any time, and it is not dependent upon any historic event occurring before it can happen, believers are also encouraged to be continuously ready for his appearing. "... keep this commandment without spot, blameless until our Lord Jesus Christ's appearing, which He will manifest in His own time..." (1 Timothy 6:14, 15). Therefore, whether we are physically caught up to meet the Lord in the air, or see Him after our death, the most cherished words every Christian ought to strive to hear from their loving Savior are: "Well done good and faithful servant" (Matthew 25:23).

"MY" KINGDOM COME

The primary problem the groups that we mentioned have with the rapture is that they all, with some variations, believe that Jesus cannot return until Christians take dominion over the planet. It's claimed that man lost the right to rule when Adam and Eve first sinned. That right was therefore yielded to Satan. The objective of Christianity, then, is to win back dominion from the devil and his demon and human followers. Many Kingdom/Dominion proponents believe the process has already begun in restoring the earth physically and morally to its original Garden of Eden state. Some claim that "manifest Sons (and Daughters) of God" are being raised up, having immortality and supernatural powers to accomplish the task. Once the kingdom is readied, and only then, they say, can Jesus come back to rule and reign.

While the Kingdom/Dominion, et al approach is positive, optimistic, and victory inspiring, it is also not Biblical. The only dominion given to man in the book of Genesis was over the sea and land animals (1:26, 28). And that dominion was reconfirmed by God to Noah after the flood (Genesis 9:1-3) — we have yet to lose it.

Nearly the entire book of Revelation denies a major victory scenario being carried out by Christians themselves prior to the return of the Lord. Victory comes only when Jesus Christ personally takes charge: "Then comes the end, when He delivers the Kingdom to God the Father, when He puts an end to all [rebellious] rule and all authority and power" (1 Corinthians 15:24). "Now out of His mouth goes a sharp sword, that with it He should strike the nations. And He Himself will rule them with a rod of iron. He Himself treads the winepress of the fierceness and wrath of Almighty God" (Revelation 19:15).

In our opinion the Kingdom/Dominion movements, which have attracted millions of true believers, are on a disasterous course. In trying to restore the earth and set up a global kingdom prior to the physical return of Jesus Christ, they are right in line with both the preparation for, and the goal of the substitute Messiah, the Antichrist.

HOW THEN SHOULD WE LIVE?

This book has attempted to give the reader a basic Biblical understanding concerning the beliefs, teachings and events sweeping across the world today. We believe it is important for all of us to know such things so that we are not included among those swept away. Believers who get caught up in false teachings, movements and programs are, at best, spinning their wheels in unproductiveness, and at worst, forfeiting God's much needed grace in their lives (Jonah 2:8 NIV). They do not lose eternal life which is not dependent on their works (Ephesians 2:8,9), but their effectiveness for the Lord can be stifled and their temporal lives ruined as they go astray. In addition to keeping ourselves on track with the Lord, the knowledge of what is going on is also tremendously helpful in rescuing others from the major deceptions of the times.

But there is an even more important purpose for understanding the times. Discerning what is taking place in the world today is critical for our effective preparation for the most glorious event that can happen in any believer's lifetime: Maranatha — Jesus' coming for us.

THE MARANATHA PREPARATION

There was an important reason for asking earlier if the thought of Jesus returning got you excited. It has everything to do with what Christianity claims to be and is. Many people who call themselves Christians do not understand that Christianity is not a religion...meaning a system of rules and rituals to aid individuals to work their way up to the acceptance and presence of God. People have that idea because that's what all religions are — except Biblical Christianity. We say Biblical because there are a lot of non-Biblical Christianities around. We also say Biblical because the Bible is the only basis for knowing what Christianity truly is.

GETTING BACK TO BASICS

All of what Christianity represents is embodied in the person of Jesus Christ. A Christian is one who has a personal relationship with the person of Jesus Christ. "... he who loves Me will be loved by My Father, and I will love him and manifest Myself to him"; "If anyone loves Me, he will keep My word; and My Father will love him, and We will come to him and make Our home with him" (John 14:21; 14:23). We can have a personal relationship with Him because He, unlike the dead founders of religions, rose from the dead and lives today. He is our living Savior. He lives in us. "Christ in you, the hope of glory" (Colossians 1:27). The "Lord Jesus Christ... through whom we live" (1 Corinthians 8:6).

So when considering the possibility of Jesus coming for us, do you react the same as you would to the arrival of a loved one? And not just any loved one, but one who is your very life: "When Christ who is our life appears, then you also will appear with Him in glory"? (Colossians 3:4).

TOO MUCH EMPHASIS ON JESUS?

It's amazing that many who call themselves Christians are ill-at-ease at the mention of the name of Jesus (other than in a church service, that is), even preferring not to talk about the One who is supposed to mean more to them than any other person. Some professing Christians who are uninformed feel that "too much" emphasis upon Him is even slighting God. But Jesus is God!

John, referring to Jesus as the Word, writes: "In the beginning was the Word, and the Word was with God, and the Word was God. He was in the beginning with God" (John 1:1,2). The Bible, from Genesis to Revelation, declares there is only one God. But God consists of three persons: the Father, the Son and the Holy Spirit. All co-equal. All one God. Jesus is God who became a man for our salvation, so that we might enter into a personal relationship with Him. "And the Word became flesh and dwelt among us" (John 1:14).

Jesus made His Divinity clear to the Jewish religious establishment which rejected Him. They complained, "... [Jesus] said that God was His Father, making Himself equal with God" (John 5:18). Jesus declared to them, "I and My Father are one," and they understood His statement, angrily replying: "You, being a Man, make Yourself God" (John 10:30; 10:33). Jesus said to a disciple, "He who has seen Me has seen the Father; so how can you say, 'Show us the Father'?" (John 14:9). Jesus the Man is God. He is the only Man who can ever truthfully proclaim His Godhood. "He is the image of the invisible God"; "For in Him dwells all the fullness of the Godhead in bodily form" (Colossians 1:15; 2:9). Being fully God and fully Man, only through Him can we get to know God personally. "If anyone loves Me, he will keep my word; and My Father will love him, and We will come to him and make Our home with him" (John 14:23).

GETTING TO KNOW HIM

Jesus said, "I have come that they may have life, and that they may have it more abundantly" (John 10:10). The abundant life is the fulfilled life, and it can only be found and fulfilled in Him. It begins with our spiritual birth. When a person first turns to Jesus Christ in faith, and trusts in Him alone for salvation, he is born again spiritually. Jesus said to a leader of the Jews, "... unless one is born again, he cannot see the kingdom of God. ... unless one is born of water [physical birth] and the [Holy] Spirit, he cannot enter the kingdom of God. ... Do not marvel that I said to you, 'You must be born again'" (John 3:3,5,7).

The Holy Spirit enters the believer and gives life to our spirit. He is given to us as a guarantee, a deposit sealing or securing us for eternity (2 Corinthians 1:22; 5:5; Ephesians 1:13,14). He takes up residence within us and empowers us to live the abundant life in Christ (Romans 8:11; 2 Corinthians 3:18). Without the help of Christ's Spirit, no one can live a life pleasing to God. As someone said, "The Christian life is as easy as walking on water." Peter accomplished that for a brief time, but only as he looked to Jesus was he enabled (Matthew 14:28-31). It is the same with us as we attempt in our own strength to "walk worthy of the Lord, fully pleasing Him, being fruitful in every good work..." (Colossians 1:10). That is impossible without His Spirit personally working in us.

It is only through God the Holy Spirit, the third person of the Godhead, that we can personally know Jesus Christ: "But when the Helper [Holy Spirit] comes, whom I shall send to you from the Father ... He will testify of Me" (John 15:26). "... no one can [truly] say that Jesus is Lord except by the Holy Spirit" (1 Corinthians 12:3). And it is the Bible, called "the sword of the Spirit" (Ephesians 6:17), which is our chief resource for getting to know Him.

HE'S IN (AND HE IS) THE WORD

The entirety of the Holy Scriptures is the revelation of Jesus Christ. You get to know about Him through reading His Word. The Old Testament is all about His first coming. Jesus, the sacrificial Lamb of God, said to the Jewish leaders, "For if you believed Moses, you would believe Me; for he wrote about Me" (John 5:46). In Genesis when God said, "Let Us make man in Our image, according to Our likeness" (1:26), the plural pronouns are referring to the three Persons of the one and only God: the Father, the Son, and the Holy Spirit.

Jesus Christ "was with God" and "was God" and "was in the beginning with God." His name means the Anointed Savior of God.

The New Testament deals with Jesus' finished sacrifice on the cross for the sins of mankind, the ministry of His Spirit in the lives of believers, and His second coming. Reading about Him is essential, but it is also necessary to know Him personally. Just as one can read up on all the facts regarding another person, unless there is some personal feedback you may feel like you know the person, but no relationship is involved. It's all one sided.

BY HIS SPIRIT

Jesus, by His Spirit, provides the personal feedback. He speaks primarily through His Word to those who believe in Him. He opens such hearts and minds to the things of His heart. He gives us understanding of His words (John 15:15). They are His words. All of the Scriptures penned by the original writers were inspired by His Spirit (2 Peter 1:20,21), and it is only through the Holy Spirit enabling us that we can truly understand them or do them (1 Corinthians 2:2-16). He causes God's Word to come alive, bearing fruit in our lives (2 Corinthians 3:6). Therefore, if we want to grow in our relationship with Jesus we have to spend time in the Scriptures, trusting in His Spirit to nurture that relationship along.

HIS WORD: KNOWING WHAT PLEASES HIM

The aim of this book has been to point again, and again, and again to the Word of God. The reason is spiritually indispensable and both temporally and eternally practical: "All Scripture is given by inspiration of God, and is profitable for doctrine, for reproof, for correction, for instruction in righteousness, that the man of God may be complete, thoroughly equipped for every good work" (2 Timothy 3:16,17). The Bible contains what Jesus wants us to know and to do. In it are all the ingredients necessary for the abundant life He promised us in Him, and He personally helps us put them together.

If we are truly His, then we are His disciples. His Word for us, therefore, is central. "If you abide in My word, you are My disciples indeed" (John 8:31). A true disciple is one who ought always be learning from and growing in the Master. His Word is the chief source of His relationship with us. Again, His Word being the things He wants us to know and to do. That is crucial. What kind of relationship can the Lord have with someone who ignores the things He knows are necessary for a good relationship?

LOVE IS THE FOUNDATION

The motivation to do the things that please Jesus and cause the relationship to grow is love: "If anyone loves Me, he will keep My word"; "He who has My commandments and keeps them, it is he who loves Me. And he who loves Me will be loved by My Father, and I will love him and manifest Myself to him"; "If you keep My commandments, you will abide in My love" (John 14:23; 14:21; 15:10). Such commandments are based on the law of love. We do what Jesus wants us to do because of our love for Him. We know the things He says are good. We know they are beneficial. We know they are true. But we are to do them because He loves us and we love Him.

"For this is the love of God, that we keep His commandments. And His commandments are not burdensome" (1 John 5:3). They are not burdensome because He bears our burdens. Paul wrote, "To this end I also labor, striving according to His working which works in me mightily" (Colossians 1:29). God's love and "His working in us" are available to make our relationship grow. The question that each of us who claims to be a follower of Christ has to answer, however, is — "Am I working at, and growing in, my relationship with Him?"

LETTERS FROM ONE WHO IS COMING SOON

If you have ever had a friend go away, someone who was very special to you, and your only source of contact was the mail, do you remember how excited you were when a letter came from that person? It's amazing how many times a letter like that gets read. It is also interesting that, though you may not call or see that friend for years, the letters that arrive from time to time keep the relationship growing. The more the person writes about himself or herself—likes, dislikes, problems, silly things, work, vacations, relationships with others, etc. — the better you know that person and, even though a great distance separates you, the closer you feel to him or her.

But let's say that one day a telegram arrives from your friend. It's agonizingly brief: "Homeward bound. Via ship. Ready or not, here I come." Nevertheless, you are overjoyed at the news. Your mind races over possibilities of arrival, but there's not enough information. No date. No trip schedule. No indication when or from what port your friend sailed. And to add to the dilemma, the telegram messenger apologetically tells you the telegram got lost and he's delivering it two weeks late. The day of arrival could be any time now.

No doubt each day would be filled with great expectation, and things to do. Lots of preparation in order to make a good impression: getting your home/apartment ready, and sprucing up yourself as well. Certainly those changes and your enthusiasm will be noticed, giving you the opportunity to talk about your friend with others. A few might share in your excitement, also looking forward to meeting your friend. There could even be some mental preparation taking place. As the days pass you go back over the stack of letters you saved to refresh your mind of some of the things your friend shared, reminding you of his or her likes and dislikes, unique qualities, and ultimately how much you miss that special person. The more you read, the more you "can't wait." Every knock at the door causes your heart to race.

THE EXPECTANT SERVANT AND THE LOVING MASTER'S RETURN

Jesus told this parable: "Be prepared — all dressed and ready — for your lord's return .... Then you will be ready to open the door and let him in the moment he arrives and knocks. There will be great joy for those who are ready and waiting for his return. He himself will seat them and ... serve them as they sit and eat! He may come at nine o'clock at night — or even at midnight. But whenever he comes there will be joy for his servants who are ready!" (Luke 12:35-38 LB).

The expectation of His coming ought to be the continuous joy of every Christian. The final thoughts in the last book of God's Word seem to almost shout out such encouragement. "Behold, I am coming quickly!" "And the Spirit and the bride say, 'Come!' And let him who hears say, 'Come!'" "He [Jesus] who testifies of these things says, 'Surely I am coming quickly.' Amen. Even so, come, Lord Jesus!" (Revelation 22:7; 22:17; 22:20).

ARE YOU READY?

Notes

Chapter 9 — Delusion and Confusion

1. *L'Oservatore Romano*, February 10, 1986, 'Spiritual Vision of Man', p. 5.

2. *Family Weekly*, Ventura Star Free Press, April 15, 1984, Cover story.

3. Dave Hunt, *Beyond Seduction* (Harvest House, 1987) p. 52, Dave Hunt and T.A. McMahon, *The Seduction of Christianity* (Harvest House, 1985), pp. 82-84, 218-220.

4. For a thorough treatment of this subject, see: H. Wayne House/Thomas Ice, *Dominion Theology: Blessing or Curse?* (Multnomah Press, 1988), Dave Hunt, *Whatever Happened to Heaven?* (Harvest House, 1988). Albert James Dagger, *Vengeance Is Ours: The Church In Dominion* (Sword Publishers, 1990).

Chapter 11— Signs Of The Times

1. "The Summit: A Nuclear Age Drama," A Public Broadcasting System presentation on the eve of Gorbachev's 1987 Washington Summit, December 1987.

Chapter 12 — Preparation For The Substitute Messiah

1. Jacob Needleman, 'Psychology and the Sacred.' *Consciousness: Brain, States of Awareness, and Mysticism.* Daniel Goleman and Richard Davidson, eds. (New York: Harper & Row, 1979), pp. 209-210.

2. Daniel Goleman, 'An Eastern Toe in the Stream of Consciousness,' *Psychology Today*, January 1981, p. 84.

Chapter 13 — The Broad Path To The Lie

1. *Time*, November 10, 1986, Richard N. Ostling, 'A Summit For Peace in Assisi,' pp. 58-59.

2. James Reid, *Ernest Holmes: The First Religious Scientist* (Science of Mind Publications, Los Angeles), p. 14.

Chapter 14 — New Species For A New Age

1. *Geo*, February 1982, 'GeoConversation,' Interview with Dr. Robert Jastrow, p. 14.

2. Jean Houston, *The Possible Human*, (J.P. Tarcher, Inc., New York, 1982), pp. 102-110.

Chapter 18 — The Maranatha Preparation

1. Dave Hunt, *The Cult Explosion*, (Harvest House, 1980), pp. 44-45.

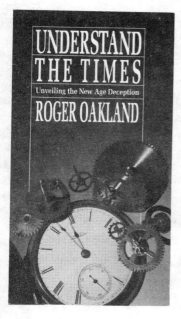